The
Natural
GARDENER

Contents

Introduction

GARDENERS TODAY ARE VERY CONCERNED ABOUT CONSERVING
THE ENVIRONMENT AND ENCOURAGING WILDLIFE — BUT MANY
ARE UNSURE JUST HOW TO GO ABOUT IT

I didn't set out to become a natural gardener. There wasn't a blinding conversion on the road to a modern Damascus. I've gardened since I was a small child and I've been moulded by my experiences. Natural gardening slowly penetrated my soul, starting with my clumsy attempts to collect cabbage white caterpillars at the age of two or three. Those early-morning forays, designed (by my grandmother) to exhaust an energetic toddler, gave me the opportunity to watch bumblebees as they robbed the nectar from the spurs at the back of aquilegias. It was one of the many mesmerizing sights I witnessed at flower height and the sense of wonder I gained then has never left me. Watching the movement and activity of insects above flowers and listening to the faint drone of a bee is still a thrill today.

In my early twenties after leaving college, having failed to get a job as a teacher, I started work at the National Vegetable Research Station. This was known by its initials NVRS and laughingly dubbed the 'envy our rest' by our small, bubbly department (say it a few times and you'll get the joke). While there, I was equipped with some high-tech equipment – a white coat and a children's paintbrush – and one of my tasks was to tickle aphids under the chin. These fragile creatures have a tube (a stylet) with which they pierce soft plant material. While looking down a microscope, I had to persuade them to remove their stylets from one plant and, with the aid of the brush, lift them to another plant. In doing so I hoped to transfer the virus from the infected plant to another large-leaved plant. This process allowed us to study and extract the virus more easily. Often I failed – snap went the stylet and out cold went the aphid. But seeing the amazing beauty of an aphid, magnified a hundred times, does make you appreciate the wonder of creation.

We grew our own colonies of aphids for this purpose and I was astonished to discover that the time-honoured method of creating more aphids was to go down to the greenhouse and use a non-systemic insecticide. This killed every living insect in the greenhouse – including the predators. New aphids emerged from

Astrantia major subsp. *involucrata* 'Canneman'

the eggs on the leaves a few days later, and with no predators about they soon thrived.

This experience shaped my thinking about insecticides. How many gardeners are repeating this experience within their own gardens – spraying when they see a colony of aphids, killing the predators and ending up with more as a result? I also saw the fragile nature of the aphid, which can easily be killed by a sudden jolt at the end of a paintbrush.

My spell at the NVRS immersed me in the world of horticulture. Working there gave me lots of extra (stolen) greenhouse space for growing plants and exposed me to new ideas and plants. I became hooked on growing cottage garden flowers, as many as I could shoehorn into my garden. And in order to feed my plant frenzy my garden ended up having a succession of flowers from early spring until late into the year – not just a midsummer flutter.

My flower-packed garden proved to be a lure for insects. Hoverflies, bees, wasps, beetles and ladybirds came and stayed. Over many years I began to notice an interdependence between them and other wildlife. Blue tits, for instance, would nest and feed their young almost exclusively from insects and grubs on the Bramley apple tree, timing their brood to coincide with the blossom. If the blossom was late, the birds waited. I noticed that aphids would appear on my plants and then disappear shortly afterwards: sometimes birds or ladybirds would eat them and sometimes tiny little wasps would parasitize their soft bodies. Slugs and snails were dispatched by a ground force of newts and frogs, or eaten by the flying squad – thrushes and blackbirds. If I was lucky, a family of hedgehogs would emerge from under the shed to snuffle through the garden. They ate slugs –

and worms – and were very active at night. I realized that by packing my garden with a wide range of plants I had created my own 'living jigsaw' of plants and animal and insect life.

I didn't leave my garden to go wild, though. While the living jigsaw worked for me, I managed the garden carefully, growing and placing my plants well, and the garden looked lovely. I was gardening naturally.

I am not an entomologist or a scientist: I'm a gardener and I can only describe the concept of the living jigsaw in simple non-scientific terms. It was illustrated to me one summer's day when some children were visiting and we noticed an achillea head in one of the undisturbed patches of the garden – a seedling from *Achillea millefolium*. I was drawn towards the grey-white flowers because they had some dense patches of blackfly on them. On closer inspection (over several minutes) I noticed that ants were climbing the flower stalks – monotonously up and down – and taking the honeydew. This is the sticky goo that exudes from the rear end of aphids when they tap into the sap of a plant. They don't suck the sap – it simply runs through the body and out again, like a hose left running. A couple of adult ladybirds were enthusiastically eating some of the blackfly. As I watched them, I saw some tiny wasps hovering above and then landing on the plant – to parasitize the blackfly. Later that day I saw a nesting pair of blue tits visiting the achillea and also eating the blackfly.

In nature everything interacts in this way, as a complex web of life. The science of ecology is built upon this fact. But although these interactions are going on underneath our eyes we don't see them. I've been astounded by the plant portraits I've taken for this book. Many of them have contained an insect that I didn't notice at the time, as well as the flower. We as gardeners simply don't notice the process when it works well – and it works best when left to its own devices, helped and managed by us.

I began to encourage other gardeners to garden naturally, but they were sceptical. And when I started to contribute to a radio phone-in, I became aware that gardeners were being urged by 'experts' to opt for a quick (commercially profitable) chemical solution whenever a problem arose. This spell on 'Spray It', as I renamed the radio show, heightened my concern about the way some gardeners are destroying their living jigsaw by repeatedly breaking the chain. If this keeps happening, some elements of that chain will disappear for ever.

In order to encourage the living jigsaw, your garden has to sustain and shelter wildlife throughout the year. You can't have a garden that is a riot of summer colour and then a bare desert during winter – if you did, your wildlife would decamp. Instead you must create a garden for all seasons, with areas of interest throughout the year. My flowering year, for instance, starts under the Bramley apple tree in February with snowdrops and hellebores and ends in late October with my autumn border.

Imagine a large Christmas tree with electric lights – the sort that light up in sequence rather than all together. As each Christmas light shines it brings part of the tree to life. To garden naturally, your garden has to light up in one area and then fade, to be replaced by another.

My own modest plot

I have a natural garden – a flower-filled garden full of healthy plants, in which I have never used a spray, a slug pellet or anything that would alter or destroy the environment. As a result wildlife abounds – particularly insect life. This book follows a year in my garden and explains the strategies I use to attract my living jigsaw of helpers. Each chapter covers a simple natural principle and describes an insect or a creature's role, from the gardener's – not the scientist's – perspective. I hope to show you how it is possible to work within these principles and create a natural garden that is not only wildlife-friendly but also beautiful. I don't want to be prescriptive and dictatorial and imply that you should take on board every strategy and principle I mention, but by giving you my recipe for my garden, Homefield, I hope to give you the courage to take that first important step towards making a natural garden.

Don't think that you have to have a country garden: you will be able to cultivate your own living jigsaw even if you live in a town or a large city. You only have to examine a piece of waste ground in an urban area to realize that nature reclaims such sites very effectively. My childhood 'botanizing' (more plant spotting, really) in London took me to derelict building sites, river banks, canal towpaths, allotment holdings and wild churchyards – where I saw lots of wildflowers and small animal life. One only has to listen to the birdlife in a London square, or see the green patchwork of garden and parkland beneath you when you arrive by plane at Heathrow, to realize that urban areas can provide important refuges for wildlife.

I've gardened at Homefield for over fifteen years. My modest, ⅓ acre (0.12 hectare) garden (gardened entirely by me on a shoestring budget) is set in a village on the north-eastern edge of the Cotswolds. Although this sounds idyllic, from a gardening point of view it's far from it. There are two main drawbacks to gardening here: stony soil and low rainfall.

My village, Hook Norton, sits on a narrow seam of ironstone that runs from north to south. This mass of stone is never far away from the soil surface. My first experience of planting here was a saga which began with a trowel and ended in blood, sweat and tears and a trip into Chipping Norton to buy a pickaxe. Said pickaxe now lies in two pieces after one plant too many. Planting anything here takes a lot of time and preparation.

Though the mass of loose stone makes planting tiresome, the main effect is that the soil is very shallow and drains freely. This makes it possible to get on the soil quickly following heavy rain – an advantage most gardeners on clay would die for. However, in the shallow soil the plants take a couple of years to get going and some never do. The thick slab of stone that underpins the garden also acts as a large storage heater; it belts out the heat in summer and cools down to a block of ice during winter. This 'block' effect makes for a slow start for spring-flowering plants and once the summer sun strikes the soil everything endures a blast of heat at the root. Mediterranean aromatic and silver-leaved plants adore it, but most roses frazzle.

The village lies in the eastern lee of the Cotswolds, which means that the rain clouds are generally empty when they get here. Hidcote Manor Garden (on the west-facing scarp, in Gloucestershire) gets every drop going, much to the chagrin of the head gardener, Glyn Jones. Chipping Norton will get a fair share too. But here, it is almost non-existent. This helps to dry the washing, but moisture-loving plants wilt. Generally our rainfall emulates East Anglia; in some years it's as little as 19 inches (50 cm).

I'm not complaining – my south-facing garden laps up the sunshine. And gardening is all about dealing with the set of conditions you have and making the best of them. To do so you must learn to look at your garden carefully. For instance, within my sun-baked, rather dry garden I have moist soil tucked against stone walls, damp corners by a west-facing wall, dry shade under dense shrubs and dappled shade under my past-its-best Bramley apple tree. Likewise your garden, however small, will contain some different areas.

The skill in gardening successfully is to go with what you've got, exploit each area and overcome difficulties creatively – choosing your plants accordingly. I have turned my sun-all-day area into a gravel garden that explodes with sun-loving flowers in early summer. The no-sun borders against the stone wall are good for ferns and ivies, which provide leafy interest for most of the year. The dappled shade under the Bramley apple tree is perfect for spring-flowering woodlanders: they thrive in its benign presence. I've also created more shade by placing wooden fences and trellises running from north to south. The eastern side of these man-made barriers gets sunshine for most of the day, but the fences shield the sun from the western aspect, and as a result this area only picks up a tiny bit of sun during midsummer evenings. These barriers allow me to grow a different range of plants on each side of them and to put a seasonal stamp on each aspect. The shady side is planted up with spring-flowering clematis, wood anemones, aquilegias and violas. It is perfect for leafy green plants, while the sunnier side is perfect for sun-loving silvers.

The cottage garden border reaches a peak in early July. The woodland garden (under the apple tree) is full of spring-flowering plants.

WINTER

CHAPTER ONE

The Spirit of the Green Man

CREATE SOME LEAFY SHELTER DURING WINTER

M id-winter sun, when it shines, is at its lowest trajectory, always catching the sides of trunks and the shapes and contour of branches. This is the time when you notice subtleties. The patchwork of algae on my apple trunk is a textured mosaic of olive, grey and brown, like a camouflaged animal. The corkscrew twists on the contorted hazel (*Corylus avellana* 'Contorta') catch every raindrop, and they glisten and tremble. The intricate marbling on the leaf of the autumn-flowering cyclamen (*C. hederifolium*) stands out against the bare earth. Everything is intensely clear in this sharp light and such glimpses can be breathtaking.

Almost everything in the garden is reduced to a bare minimum. The occasional bolts of rich evergreen leaf are the only solid touches of warmth; they glow and lift our spirits. It's obvious why our pagan ancestors worshipped these plants, the hollies and ivies, as potent symbols of everlasting life. These patches of green leaf add structure and form as well as strong colour, and they are an essential element in a natural garden, as leafy plants provide a hiding place for birds, mammals, spiders and insects, sometimes for hibernation, sometimes purely for shelter.

A large evergreen tree or shrub spreads a canopy over the ground that provides a dry, warm place at ground level. It also shields the garden from the prevailing wind, creating a warmer subclimate within – and a sheltered garden will attract more wildlife throughout the year. If these leafy plants bear fruit during winter, so much the better, as the fruit will feed the birds.

A garden 'put to bed' in late September is a drab affair during the winter months when only huge expanses of brown soil and twig survive. Worse still, if you create a garden where every plant dies back to the bare earth you expose all living things to winter hardship and they will move away to more sheltered climes. The natural gardener must compromise. You will need to

Previous page *Ilex aquifolium*
Left *Euphorbia amygdaloides* 'Craigieburn', the best cultivar of our native wood spurge

meticulously tidy some areas, those containing spring bulbs for instance, but in other places leave the garden tidy-up until early spring. In the areas that do demand an autumn tidy, it's worth making piles of woody stems at the back of the border for insect, amphibian and small mammal cover, which you can carefully move in mid-spring. Other areas – hedge bottoms for instance – must be left well alone as leaf litter provides excellent shelter for small mammals, bees, spiders and insects.

The natural gardener needs to plant some evergreens on the boundaries, use yew and box for winter structure, and add some evergreen climbers. At ground level, growing herbaceous plants with good winter leaves is very desirable. By doing this you will have a green presence that is aesthetically warming as well as being a protective environment.

Hollies

Holly is one of the most useful evergreens for the natural gardener – a plant that provides food and shelter on one bush. Ensuring that a holly produces berries needs some contrivance because most forms have flowers of only one sex on each plant. Plants like these are called dioecious (literally meaning two houses) and usually pollen needs to pass between a male plant and a female plant before berries can be formed. A few forms of holly are able to perform by themselves: *Ilex aquifolium* 'J.C. van Tol' is self-fertile and 'Pyramidalis' has the ability to form fruit in the absence of pollination, which makes them desirable where space is limited.

Three hollies along the fern walk:
Top *Ilex aquifolium* 'Handsworth New Silver'
Centre *I. x altaclerensis* 'Silver Sentinel' (syn. 'Belgica Aurea')
Bottom *I. x a.* 'Golden King'

Most hollies, then, need a partner of the opposite sex to make berries. The names of hollies are often misleading. 'Silver Queen' is in fact a drag queen of the plant world, being male. There are three ways round this. The *RHS Plant Finder* records the sex of all the hollies listed and also indicates whether the foliage is variegated. *The Hillier Manual of Trees and Shrubs* will also tell you, as will a specialist nursery. However, if you live in a rural district with lots of wild hollies growing close by, having a married couple within the garden walls may not be as necessary, as the bees will flirt between the wild and cultivated forms.

Our native holly, *Ilex aquifolium*, gets its species name from *aquila*, Latin for eagle, and the spines are extremely sharp, like the tip of an eagle's talon. Forms of *I. aquifolium* cannot be accommodated within a border – unless you want lacerated fingers every time you weed. You can tuck them on the boundary edges of the garden to great effect, or plant them as specimens in a lawn. Female forms of this spiny holly can be heavily berried. 'Handsworth New Silver', a smartly variegated cream and green, 'Madame Briot', a brash mottled dark yellow and green, and 'Golden Milkmaid', green and gold, all form red berries. There are yellow-berried forms too, such as 'Bacciflava'. Growth habits vary widely in *I. aquifolium*: some make handsome, tree-shaped pyramids while others barely leave the ground – so do your research carefully before you plant, checking habit as well as sex.

A chance cross between our native (*I. aquifolium*) and an imported exotic, tender holly from the Azores (*I. perado*) produced a large-leaved holly with an open, airy habit and leaves kinder to gardeners' hands. This hybrid, *Ilex × altaclerensis,* is also called Highclere holly because it was first found growing at Highclere Castle near Newbury, Berkshire, in 1838. There are now many forms and you can use these within a border as the oval leaves are much less savage to the touch than those of *I. aquifolium*. They make handsome shrubs, but are never heavily laden with berries. *I. × altaclerensis* 'Silver Sentinel' (syn. 'Belgica Aurea') has mottled grey and green leaves edged with creamy-white margins. 'Lawsoniana' has a much brighter leaf irregularly splashed with yellow, and 'Camelliifolia' has large, rounded, dark green leaves. All bear red berries held in ones and twos.

Hollies are slow-growing shrubs that are best planted when young. Water plants regularly during the first growing season. Once established, hollies survive well on light, dry soil. If you have a small garden, you can use two or three hollies in topiarized forms. Leave the holly to establish for at least a season before you begin to snip – late spring or early summer are the best times. Topiarized hollies will not berry as freely, but they make denser cover.

Yew versus leylandii

Gardeners tend to associate yew hedges with great gardens such as Hidcote and Sissinghurst. Countless articles have sold us the idea that Leyland cypress (× *Cupressocyparis leylandii*) is the fast-growing hedging option for the ordinary gardener and have brainwashed us against using 'slow-to-grow' yew. Now, however, the curse of the leylandii is coming home to roost. I have spent

Taxus baccata 'Fastigiata', the slender columnar yew

and the area dries out under the network of fibrous roots. The biggest drawback is that past-their-best leylandii have brown skirts at the base when they mature. They don't have the ability to reshoot from bare wood. However, when I removed my hedge, section by section, the birdlife (particularly the finches) disappeared with it and on reflection I wish I'd kept one or two for shelter.

Yew (*Taxus baccata*) is more expensive than leylandii, but planted in good soil and fed regularly (with a water-soluble plant food every month during the growing season) it will form a 4 foot (1.2 metres) high hedge within six years or so. Should it get away as a result of a few years of neglect (as if Sleeping Beauty is near by), it can resprout after a chainsaw massacre, from bare wood. If you inherit such an overgrown castle, prune back the sunny side of the yew first, cutting back the top to the required height, and when that side is strongly growing back tackle the other side, taking it down to the first side's level.

There are differing forms of yew – columnar, plump, slow-growing hedging varieties and golden-leaved – and, like the holly, there are male and female plants. By planting a pair of yew trees or a screen you create a leafy place for insects, food for birds and an easily maintained architectural feature – one slow-growing enough to survive some neglect. The flesh-covered seeds of the yew rarely last beyond mid-November in my garden. Indeed one of my autumn rituals is to watch the blackbirds stripping them from a pair of Irish yews (*T. b.* 'Fastigiata') while I lie in bed and drink tea. (A bungalow does have some advantages.) Like yo-yos these eager birds bob up and down as they feed. These

five years eradicating the 40 foot (12 metre) high leylandii belt which towered above me from every boundary – a barrier I inherited when I moved here and one I couldn't maintain with a pair of hand-held shears and a ladder.

A leylandii hedge needs a yearly August cut. Sadly, once these trees escape from a yearly crewcut, they leap skywards. Left for longer, they cover a swathe of soil with their girth – in my case 20 feet (6 metres) of garden border –

fastigiate yews are the only yews I have and I'm pledged to bend them into an arch – but given my time again I would have planted a yew screen along part of my boundary. Yew is also the perfect foil for summer-flowering perennials.

Box

Like yew, the box tree (*Buxus sempervirens*) is slow-growing, long-lived, hardy and easily manageable. It is the other great mainstay of the large traditional garden, the plant most used to form a parterre or small topiary. The required yearly trim was traditionally performed on Derby Day in early June, when house guests were away at the races. By then the last of the severe frosts – which could reduce the new growth to a brown mess – had passed.

I haven't aspired to a box parterre – not only because it would hardly match my 1920s bungalow but also because I once witnessed a severe, midsummer haircut along an overgrown box hedge and this 36 inch (90 cm) high 'scruff' harboured more snails than I've ever seen or ever want to see again. Also, the horticultural nightmare of planting the areas inside a box parterre causes head gardeners sleepless nights because the surface-rooting box leaches out the moisture from the surrounding soil with a network of tiny roots. Parterres usually rely upon bulbs and annuals (grown from sprinkled seeds) for seasonal colour.

Parterres apart, though, if you like leafy gardens it is worth having box in your garden. I use the plain *Buxus sempervirens*, leaving it to form its natural egg-shape and then neatening it. The trees merge in summer, lost in the froth

A box-lined border in a London garden

of leaf, but reappear in the winter to form welcome blobs of green. There are also blue-green forms (*B.s.* 'Blauer Heinz'), compact forms (*B. microphylla* 'Green Pillow') and upright columns (*B. sempervirens* 'Handsworthiensis').

The golden-leaved *Lonicera nitida* 'Baggesen's Gold' is often vaunted as a good substitute for topiarized box. Experience has taught me that this sends up tall spindly shoots and therefore needs clipping every month during summer. In mild winters it grows on unabated. Box survives with one clip – two at most – and the new growth is uniform.

Containerized box is often used in small gardens, but it needs constant watering during summer and good nutrition (with a soluble plant food every two weeks) to keep its rich gloss and avoid that burnished, metallic olive-tree shimmer. It's only worth the trouble in a small town garden or in a garden where help is plentiful.

Ivies grow where little else dares

Ivies are versatile performers. They can scale a fence, cover a ledge or stand erect, and the variety of leaf shape, habit and colour makes them useful in a garden – for both cover and beauty. Unfortunately they (like box) are snail catchers. Snails cluster together in large colonies at this time of year, hidden behind containers, wall shrubs or winter-flowering irises. January is an excellent time to poke about and find their hiding places. I once removed a football-sized clump of forty or so (sealed solidly together) after finding them at the back of a large stand of *Iris unguicularis*.

There are hundreds of different forms of common ivy (*Hedera helix*). I use several of the smaller varieties as ground cover, to soften steps or cover ground near ferns. 'Anita', 'Duckfoot' and 'Ivalace' are well-behaved, decorative green-leaved ivies I particularly favour. These three cover the ground – they won't climb.

I don't cover fences or walls with forms of *H. helix* as its adventitious roots penetrate the mortar or panels. The shoots also head into the eaves of a house, building or shed. The larger-leaved ivies (*H. algeriensis* (*H. canariensis* of gardens) and *H. colchica*) climb without adventitious roots. They need wire supports, but are much less damaging to walls and fences.

Ivies are useful in two ways. First, they will grow in the darkest places, underneath trees for instance, where grass gives up the ghost. Strangely, though, the completely golden-leaved forms (such as *H. helix* 'Buttercup') need good light to develop their golden colours. Second, ivies provide nectar-rich flowers late in the year. *H. helix*, when left to its own devices, bears two different forms of foliage – juvenile and adult. The juvenile foliage climbs and has typically ivy-shaped leaves. If left to grow, the adult foliage, which is often oval in leaf, stands upright and the branches are woody or arborescent. These branches bear umbels of sickly-sweet flowers during November, which lure and sustain many flies and other insects. By January, the berries have turned from green to black. Birds eat them only in hard winters, as a fall-back, but ivies provide good sites for early nesting birds – the blackbird and the robin. If your garden is large enough to contain a fruiting ivy it will pull in birds, insects and spiders.

More good evergreens

A visit to a garden centre or nursery during the winter months will reveal several other shrubs with good evergreen leaves – though most do not have an abundant crop of fruit or berry. There is an amazing choice of conifers of different sizes, shapes, foliage colour and preferred soil type, which you should incorporate into your garden for structural effect and for wildlife reasons. Here are some evergreens I use in the shady edges of my garden:

Large evergreens for shady boundaries

Aucuba japonica 'Crotonifolia' is a handsome evergreen, rather like an irregularly spotted laurel, which enjoys shade and makes a good boundary plant against a fence.

Elaeagnus pungens 'Maculata' has oval leaves which have a central splash of brightish gold on a dark green leaf. Where the colours overlap, an irregular margin of olive green frames the central splash. This handsome shrub has one bad habit: it reverts to plain green leaves at the drop of a hat and needs careful watching. As with any variegated shrub, cut off any plain green shoots before they take over.

Viburnum tinus produces heads of tiny flowers from November until March. These flowers open white but emerge from rose-pink buds, and this combination, framed by the plain oval green leaves, is unbeatable in the winter garden. The flowers don't have the powerful fragrance of many winter- and spring-flowering viburnums but this luxuriant, feminine shrub will flower in shade, giving the boundary a full softness. 'Gwenllian' is the prettiest to my eyes.

Mahonia japonica has long racemes of fragrant lemon-yellow flowers which hang downwards from the upper parts of the shrub. The pinnate leaves are quite spiny, but this mahonia will flower at the back of a border in full shade, so you won't have to brush past it. There are many fine cultivars of mahonia, including the favourite *M. × media* 'Charity'.

Aucuba japonica 'Crotonifolia'

Smaller evergreens for dappled shade

You can plant the areas of the garden that get a mixture of sun and shade with some smaller evergreens. *Euonymus fortunei* 'Silver Queen' is a small shrub with green leaves edged with a creamy-white margin. There are also variegated golden-leaved sorts ('Emerald Gaiety') and all-green sorts as well – 'Emerald Charm', for instance.

Winter leaves

Several herbaceous plants also provide leaves during winter:

Most verbascums
All foxgloves (*Digitalis*)
Biennial thistles (*Silybum marianum* and
    Onopordum acanthium)
Evergreen kniphofias and eryngiums
Oriental poppies (*Papaver orientale*)
Corsican hellebore (*Helleborus argutifolius*)
Primrose, polyanthus, etc.
Violet (*Viola*)
Vincas
Iris foetidissima
Epimedium perralderianum
Corydalis ochroleuca
Ferns – *Polystichum* and *Polypodium*
Heucherellas, heucheras and tiarellas
Comfrey (*Symphytum*)

Using variegated leaves wisely

It's worth saying that variegated foliage comes in two colourways: cool, restrained cream and green, and brasher, warmer gold and green. This affects their use in the garden. The brasher shades are good in dark corners, the cooler creams and greens in lighter areas, but they should never (in my opinion) be mixed together. The golden forms are very good with blue and yellow flowers. The cooler creams mingle best with pinks, whites and purples. All variegated plants, whether cool or warm, should be supported by an abundance of green leaf if you're to avoid a 'measles' effect.

Top Verbascum rosette
Centre *Polystichum setiferum*
Bottom *Iris foetidissima*

Evergreen climbers

Sheltered house walls and fences can provide the perfect conditions for evergreen climbers. My warm, south-facing wall supports a Californian ceanothus, two winter-flowering clematis (*C. armandii* from China and *C. cirrhosa* found in southern Europe and Asia) with *Iris unguicularis,* an Algerian native, at the base. This mixture provides flowers from January until May, attracting the earliest bees and other insects.

Walls that face north can also be very sheltered as most of our wind and weather come from the west and south and rarely from the north. *Garrya elliptica* needs a frost-free place if its leathery grey-green leaves and catkins are to avoid being blackened by hard weather. There are two superior sorts: 'Glasnevin' has red catkins and 'James Roof' has much longer grey-green catkins – sometimes reaching 20 inches (50 cm) in length.

Another candidate for a north- or east-facing wall, *Ribes speciosum*, which comes into leaf in autumn, puts out red fuchsia-like flowers in April. The downside is that it reverts to a bare, prickly skeleton in summer. Some roses will also thrive, including the legendary 'Madame Alfred Carrière', the rose that spans the north wall at Sissinghurst in Kent.

Top Pulmonaria and foxgloves (*Digitalis purpurea*)
Bottom *Dryopteris wallichianum*

THE LADYBIRD

One of the most important insects you'll be protecting in your leafy plants during the winter months is the ladybird. Most species are predatory, both during their adult life and when they are larvae, and devour lots of aphids. Aphids are one of the pests gardeners worry about most – and with good reason. By removing the sap from plants they cause loss of vigour and spread viral diseases as they tap into the phloem. The sticky sap that leaks out of the back end of the aphid also encourages the fungal disease sooty mould, which leaves a black deposit.

Before you panic, it's worth remembering two things about aphids. Firstly they feed through a tube (the stylet) and when they're physically shaken (by hand or a jet of water) this breaks very easily, rendering them harmless. Secondly many aphids are specific feeders – that is, each species attacks a different plant. Aphids on your roses won't mean aphids on every other plant.

Encouraging ladybirds – and different parts of the country attract different species – will help prevent aphid attack, as one adult ladybird will eat 70 aphids a day. A female ladybird will lay 1,500 eggs during her lifetime – usually a year. The eggs are always laid close to colonies of aphids, in batches of 20 to 40, and one larva will eat 400 aphids before pupating.

So gardeners take note! In order to attract egg-laying ladybirds into your garden you must have some aphid colonies. Therefore gardens 'under the sprayer' won't attract ladybirds and, if they do, most of the sprays will kill them. Once you've got ladybirds you won't need to spray, as they'll hoover the aphids up at a rate. Ladybirds also eat mealy bugs, scale insects, mites and whitefly.

Therefore you must encourage ladybirds to stay and that means providing hibernation sites and leafy plants during the winter months. Then when spring arrives your ladybirds are ready and waiting. Ladybirds hibernate in different ways according to the species, but favoured places include old tree trunks, hollow stems, plant rosettes and garden debris. Hollow-stemmed plants make excellent homes – fennel stems are among their favourites.

Most ladybirds shelter close to the ground. Nettles and thistles are important sources of food, both of which have species-specific aphids, so having a small area of these will help you to sustain ladybirds early in the season. In mild winters leafy plants such as the evergreen *Euphorbia characias* and *E.* × *martinii* attract clusters of ladybirds. They also overwinter on conifer trees, box, sage, rosemary and tree lupins.

Some gardeners make ladybird houses. Using strips of wood, make a rectangular or triangular frame, pack it with hollow stems and then hang it on the wall, close to the ground, to provide shelter.

Opposite and above from left Ladybird pupa on an achillea leaf; ladybird larva; ladybird pupa

Ladybird facts

There are 5,000 different species of ladybird throughout the world. They belong to a family of beetles called Coccinellids. America boasts 400 different species. Britain alone has 46 different species. Of these, 24 would normally be recognized as ladybirds by their striking colour. This bright pigmentation is nature's way of saying 'I don't taste very nice.' For this reason ladybirds don't get eaten for breakfast by other creatures. And if attacked they have a secret weapon: they lie on their backs and squirt smelly liquid from their legs.

Our five commonest ladybirds

Seven-spot ladybird (*Coccinella septempunctata*) – the commonest ladybird, red with black spots. It often hibernates in evergreen shrubs, hollow stems, grass and dead foliage.

Two-spot ladybird (*Adalia bipunctata*) – usually has two black spots, but sometimes has four or six. These hibernate in large clusters, often close to the house, on tree trunks or on fence posts.

Ten-spot ladybird (*Adalia decempunctata*) – very variable. It is either orange or brown, and has ten or twelve small dark or reddish spots. It hibernates on the ground in twos or threes in leaf litter.

Eleven-spot ladybird (*Coccinella undecimpunctata*) – commoner near coastal regions. It has five spots on each side and one central spot close to its head.

Fourteen-spot ladybird (*Propylea quatuordecimpunctata*) – yellow with black rectangular spots. It is often found near old pastures and wooded grassland. It hibernates in twos and threes in hollow stems.

A seven-spot ladybird on a phlomis leaf

CHAPTER TWO

Winter Fragrance

PROVIDE NECTAR FOR AS MANY DAYS OF THE YEAR AS YOU CAN, ESPECIALLY DURING THE WINTER AND EARLY SPRING

Every time I fill up the log basket when the weather's mild, there's a spicy, hyacinth fragrance in the air. This comes from the tall, upright shrub overhanging the fence, *Viburnum × bodnantense* 'Dawn', each of whose twiggy branches bears clusters of pale-pink flowers. It's one of the great mysteries of gardening: how do such tiny flowers produce such a strong and powerful scent? Though I'm not sure how they manage it, I do know why they do it. They use scent to lure insects, which are necessary for pollination, and the fragrance has to be really powerful as it must carry at cool temperatures. The flower structure has to be able to survive wintry weather, which is why flowers that appear at this time of the year are often tiny and sometimes almost hidden. Large, blowzy flowers with soft petals would never survive heavy rain, sharp frost and snow.

If the afternoon is warm in late January – a time when the light levels and day length are increasing daily – there may be a large bumblebee about, lured by the distinctive scent of *V. × bodnantense* 'Dawn'. Bumblebees emerge in clement weather to top up their food supplies, as they don't have large stores of food to sustain them; the honeybee, with its elaborate hive full of sustenance, waits until late May before emerging.

The natural gardener must whenever possible provide nectar, the sugar-rich liquid that sustains bees and other insects and gives them the energy to breed and fly. Once boosted by a nectar-laden feed the predatory insects – lacewings and hoverflies – will lay their eggs close to your aphid colonies, and the larvae will prey on the aphids, keeping your plants clear of infestation. As the insects systematically go about their pleasurable task, many of them pollinate plants as a by-product of the feeding process: while an insect is looking for nectar, or pollen (which contains proteins and fats) or both, pollen from the plant which it is visiting sticks to its head or body and is thus transferred from one plant to the next it visits. Pollination ensures reproduction, which is vital in the plant

Hamamelis x intermedia 'Jelena' is totally unaffected by hard, wintry weather.

world, both for the production of fruit and seed, and for genetic diversity. Sustaining these early pollinators by providing fragrant flowers, such as the viburnum, is vital – particularly in winter and spring, as these are critical times for bumblebees.

Scented shrubs

Viburnum × *bodnantense* is one of the finest shrubs for winter fragrance, starting into flower during November while still in leaf and luring any bumblebee that may emerge. As the viburnum leaves drop, the flowers continue. Sometimes they are halted and browned by spells of cold weather and hard frost, but flushes of flower go on through March and April. Though it's too straight and large to be grown as a specimen shrub, it can be accommodated on a boundary fence, where its heavy scent can still make an impact.

Most winter and early-spring flowers are best placed close to paths and doorways, where you can inhale and appreciate them as you scurry back and forth. Viburnums are easy plants and they tolerate my limy soil well. I use two scented spring-flowering viburnums in my fern walk – a short path (30 yards/30 metres long) which skirts the back of my woodland and autumn borders. Both of these flower later than *V.* × *b.* 'Dawn' and are hybrids of *V. carlesii*, a daphne-scented May-flowering viburnum. The open airy *V.* × *burkwoodii* has a sparse number of shiny evergreen leaves which frame white flowers held in pink buds. This medium-sized shrub is earlier and taller than

Top *Viburnum* x *bodnantense* (*V. farreri* x *V. grandiflorum*)
Centre *V.* x *burkwoodii* (*V. carlesii* x *V. utile*)
Bottom *V.* x *juddii* (*V. carlesii* subsp. *carlesii* x subsp. *bitchiunense*)

my other favourite, the deciduous *V. × juddii*. This bushier plant has heads of pink-tinged flowers, slightly clove-scented. These two spring-flowering shrubs could be tucked towards the back of a border or incorporated in a woodland border. Both appear by April – sometimes earlier.

My limy soil should stop me growing a number of plants – magnolias and witch hazels among them. When I plant something that I shouldn't perhaps attempt to grow, I comfort myself with the thought that plants can't read textbooks, and it seems to work. I always advise gardeners who are desperate to grow a certain plant to have a go – but to be prepared for failure. (A good motto for life as well as gardening.) I grow, for instance, three sorts of the hybrid witch hazel (*Hamamelis × intermedia*), a delicately scented winter-flowering shrub, despite their reputed predilection for acid to neutral soil. In an attempt to placate them, I have added organic matter to my shallow soil and given them a cool root run by tucking them away at the back of a herbaceous border. Plants with Himalayan provenance seem to demand coolness at the root and rich organic matter in the soil.

Though they are at the back of the border, my witch hazels can be clearly seen from a window during the winter months; yet they can barely be seen from the lawn during summer. Tucking spring-flowering plants (shrubs, hellebores and bulbs) away like this is a useful device, especially if you make an accessible path to stroll along. During

Top *Hamamelis* x *intermedia* 'Arnold Promise'
Centre *H.* x *i.* 'Diane'
Bottom *H.* x *i.* 'Jelena'

summer we admire most flower borders from the lawn. In winter the perspective reverses – we mainly glimpse our gardens from the house or from pathways.

The hybrid witch hazels have flowers that resemble floppy spiders with citrus-peel ribbons for legs. These 'spiders' appear in January, running up bare wood, and seem able to resist the hardest weather – both cold and wet. The spicy scent (smelling it is like sniffing a bottle of astringent witch hazel from the chemist) needs considerable warmth and stillness to register on the nose. The visual delight of the flower, though, is enough for me, especially on a bleak January day. If the flowers are not enough to woo you, the hazel-shaped leaves are thickly textured (corrugated like crinkle-cut crisps) and often colour up to warm red and orange during the autumn.

You should always buy hamamelis when they are in flower – then you can see what you're getting. Reducing each leading stem by a third straight after flowering produces more flower buds on the side shoots. I have gone for three modern hybrids – *Hamamelis × intermedia* 'Arnold Promise' (a bright yellow), 'Diane' (a warm red) and 'Jelena' (a copper orange). 'Arnold Promise' – bred at the Arnold Arboretum in Massachusetts – has a profusion of small, tighter flowers late in the season. This is a disadvantage as January 'spiders' are much more desirable than late arrivals to the mid-winter ball. The other two, 'Diane' and 'Jelena', bred at the Kalmthout Arboretum in Belgium by Jelena and Robert de Belder, have larger, more ragged flowers, but there are fewer of them. The finest is 'Pallida', a pale yellow hamamelis which smells of freesias.

Though witch hazels flower reliably every year for most people, mine take a sabbatical sometimes – especially if they produce seeds. This is perhaps a sign that they would prefer less limy soil than mine.

When I gardened on the English version of the Russian steppes (aka south Northamptonshire), I contented myself with the almond-pink *Daphne mezereum*, which flowers in spring on bare wood. I dreamt and craved the choicer kinds of these fragrant plants with purple-pink, waxy flowers set against shiny, evergreen leaves – but lacked conviction. When I moved to Homefield fifteen years ago I scoured the local gardens and discovered several large floriferous daphnes within the village. (Snooping, with eye and nose, is a valuable exercise when assessing a new garden's potential.)

To thrive, daphnes need that gardening paradox of full sun and moisture-retentive soil. They also need to be planted when young and small in stature. I grow four, but I would love to have more. I have put the small evergreen *D. × burkwoodii* 'Somerset Variegated' close to the house, where it gets the warmth from the sun, helping it to release its scent. Every time anyone comes through the back gate during April, it produces a waft of perfume from its cluster of pink flowers held at the top of every branching twig. I meet its moisture-retentive demands by applying a thick gravel mulch, which I renew every third year.

Under the outer edges of the old Bramley apple tree I've placed the compact spurge laurel (*D. laureola*), a native woodlander. It produces a rosette of shiny green leaves topped with a cluster of lime-green tubular flowers, which smell sweetly on warm afternoons. This goes well

Daphne x *burkwoodii* 'Somerset Variegated' produces scented spring flowers.

with snowdrops – often flowering at the same time – and though not spectacular in spring it looks glossy and handsome throughout the year.

My other daphne, set at the edge of the Bramley's canopy, is *D. bholua* 'Jacqueline Postill', an erect evergreen of Himalayan provenance. This winter-flowering daphne is one of the hardiest forms of *D. bholua*, but it still needs the shelter of a house or a deciduous overhead tree. The all-important factor for producing the maximum scent is afternoon sunshine. In the early part of the year the morning sun is very harsh and damaging, thawing out any frosted petals and leaves far too quickly. Slow thaws – away from morning sun – are best. I have great hopes that my 'Jacqueline Postill' will make a substantial shrub in time. The heavily scented purplish pink flowers, which appear in February, mix

well with the hellebores and snowdrops growing close by.

Finally, I have tucked away the prostrate small *D. blagayana* in deep shade (where I was told to put it by the nurseryman) to provide the cool root run it needs to produce its white February flowers – said to appear by St Valentine's Day. This none-too-spectacular daphne should spread along the ground by self-layering and reach a foot or so (30 cm) high.

D. odora 'Aureomarginata', probably the easiest daphne of all, is luckily one of the most pungently scented. It is a hardy, evergreen daphne capable of doing well in light, limy soil heavily enriched with organic matter. Given shelter and afternoon sun, this short, spreading shrub will fill a small garden with its perfume. The variegated 'Aureomarginata' is hardier and flowers more freely than the ordinary *D. odora*.

Perhaps the most overpowering scent of all belongs to the sarcococca, a Chinese relative of the box family commonly called Christmas box. The flowers, which are little more than bunches of stamens, produce a lily-like fragrance which is potently heady. A 6 inch (15 cm) high plant transported in a warm car will induce nausea in the passengers and prompt them to cry, 'It's them or us.' (They won't like the reply.)

I've found sarcococcas difficult to grow in my garden: they're slow to an extreme and need very fertile soil. Instead, I tend to use them as container plants close to doors, mixed with skimmias, heathers and cyclamens. The most heavily flowered (and perfumed) is S. *hookeriana* var. *digyna* – a small, narrow-leaved shrub with red stamens.

The evergreen skimmias are not as scented as the sarcococcas, but their ability to produce conical heads of tight, round buds way before winter starts makes them very decorative plants for the winter garden and container. These buds produce April flowers adored by bees – which makes them highly useful in containers and in the garden setting. My all-time favourite, S. × *confusa* 'Kew Green', is a small shrub with evergreen leaves. By November there are tight heads of pale cream buds, which open to white by late spring. The larger S. *laureola* grows in the garden (in deep shade) and produces heads of flower from April to June.

So many gardeners have sturdy terracotta containers which they fill with tender plants during summer, but I favour winter containers, placed close to front and back door, where they benefit from the shelter of the house and lift the

Sarcococca confusa

spirits. I like to fill them with a backbone of small fragrant evergreen shrubs – skimmias and sarcococcas – planted in a soil-based compost such as John Innes No. 2. I then fill in the backbone planting with a succession of pots – bulbs, hardy cyclamens, heathers, ivies, euonymus and polyanthas. The winter containers stay put all year long, watered with the contents of my teapot during hot weather.

Close by the back door are two deep glazed containers of Christmas rose (*Helleborus niger*), a plant that does much better in a container than in bare earth. Each one puts out seventy or more large white flowers – from February onwards – which sustain the bees for weeks.

The evergreen leaves of the gentle climber *Clematis cirrhosa* have a blackish tinge and the pendent flowers, which appear here by February, are soft cream spotted with red. There are two widely available cultivars. 'Freckles' has heavily spotted creamy flowers streaked with red and larger leaves. *C.c.* var. *balearica*, the one I grow, has heavily

Left *Clematis cirrhosa* var. *balearica* enjoys a warm wall and often starts to flower close to Christmas.

divided leaves and is often known as the fern-leaved clematis. The pale greenish-yellow flowers are spotted in purple red and I prefer this, though I cannot say why. It's daintier – more subtle perhaps. It covers the wall by my large patio window and, when the flowers are out, the sleepy bees stumble into the glass.

In complete contrast to such delicacy, *C. armandii* bears lengthy, robustly leathery leaves on strong climbing stems and sinuous tendrils which are difficult to train. Mine seem to avoid the wire supports, constantly flopping over the ceanothus beneath it. The leathery leaves occasionally turn to snuff-brown paper close to the stem, ruining the look of this glossy climber. This is the nature of the plant. Pick them off! The clusters of white flowers, sheltered by the warm wall, appear in March or April and look far too exotic and waxy for a Cotswold garden in spring. Alas, my white walls do not enhance the flowers, but they

would look sumptuous against red brick. The bees are quick to find them, though – white wall or not.

All forms of clematis like to have cool roots – a situation which can be contrived on a south-facing, sunny wall by using one of three devices. You can place a large container in front of the base of an established clematis, thereby shading the roots of the plant. It's much better, though, to provide some protection when you initially plant your clematis by placing a piece of stone or paving (about 9 inches/23 cm across) just under the soil surface and above the root ball. This barrier will conserve moisture and keep the roots cool. The third way is to place a leafy plant at the base. I use the winter-flowering *Iris unguicularis* at the base of both *Clematis armandii* and *C. cirrhosa*. This iris enjoys a baking position against the base of a dry wall – the sort of conditions it would endure in its native Algeria. The flowers, usually a soft blue,

open and last a day and it's possible to pick them and watch them unfurl within a few minutes in a warm room.

South-facing red-brick walls also set off the winter jasmine, a plant whose yellow flowers are sometimes over by Christmas. *Jasminum nudiflorum* fills a unique spot during the gardening year – what else can look that fresh and gauche in November? The early *Narcissus* 'Cedric Morris' grows close to the south-facing wall of my house, close to winter-flowering irises, and is always out on New Year's Day. Another fragrant recommendation for a warm sheltered wall is the fine-leaved Chilean shrub *Azara microphylla*. The tiny yellow flowers (hidden from view) smell strongly of vanilla in early spring. It's on my 'want-to-grow' list.

If you have a dark corner, *Osmanthus delavayi* will thrive there to great effect. This large,

privet-like shrub has shiny evergreen leaves and pure white fragrant flowers along every branch and twig. It needs clipping back after flowering to avoid becoming too leggy and thin. One thrives here in one corner of the garden, backed by two fences – a most inhospitable setting. Avoid the similar *O.* × *burkwoodii* – the flowers are not as fragrant or such a clean white.

I have also found room for a winter-flowering shrubby honeysuckle, *Lonicera* × *purpusii,* thought to be a hybrid between *L. standishii* and *L. fragrantissima.* Both parents were found by Robert Fortune in China in 1865. I grow it close to a path leading to the main greenhouse. The sweetly fragrant, creamy flowers last well in water and look good in a vase with winter iris.

Above from left *Clematis armandii; Iris unguicularis* 'Mary Barnard'; *Narcissus* 'Cedric Morris'; *Lonicera* x *purpusii* 'Winter Beauty'

THE BUMBLEBEE

At the first hint of warmth – often in late January – the low drone of the bumblebee can be heard in my garden. It is probably a newly emerged queen looking for a nesting site. In order to lay her eggs she will need to find a supply of nectar to give her energy and pollen for protein – to mature the eggs in her ovaries. Once she has found a nesting site and she has enough energy she will collect and store pollen, eventually laying about six to eight eggs. To sustain her, you will need early flowers in your garden. Each generation is born at roughly six-week intervals throughout the year and the bees born earlier in the year are smaller than the bees born later in the season, when there are larger colonies and more workers to feed them.

Bumblebees can fly earlier in the year than any other bees and in cooler temperatures. The reason is that they have the ability to generate their own body heat chemically – they're warm-blooded. Honeybees (see page 114) can only fly in warm conditions. This ability to fly early in the year and in cool temperatures makes the bumblebee a vital pollinator. They also 'buzz pollinate' flowers – by buzzing they shake the flower and that releases the pollen.

When foraging, bumblebees leave a scent mark as they visit each flower and this indicates to other bees that the nectar supply there is temporarily diminished and that they should look elsewhere – saving them time. They also have the ability to travel over long distances – up to 3½ miles (6 kilometres) from the nest.

Bumblebees have a preference for tubular flowers. Among their favourites are foxgloves (*Digitalis*), aconitums and nepetas. They have a system, always working from the bottom of the spike upwards. The lower flowers have a more abundant supply of nectar than the upper ones, but the 'upper' flowers are pollen-rich. As the bee gets higher up the flower spike the nectar dries up, but pollen is abundant. The pollen is carried to the bottom of another flower spike and pollination takes place. Other flowers, like anchusa, regulate the nectar supply in individual flowers by turning it on and off in a random way – a clever device that, by making the bee search for nectar in other flowers or another plant, encourages pollination.

Comfrey with robber-bee damage at the base of the corolla tube

There are short-tongued and long-tongued bumblebees. The long-tongued bees are more specialized and can access flowers with long tubes. Though other bees might bite into the back of such flowers, doing this does not pollinate the flower – it only steals the nectar. The long-tongued bumblebees may well be the only pollinators of some flowers.

The bumblebee is an important pollinator of flowers, vegetables and fruit, especially early in the year. The following crops rely heavily on them:

Broad beans
Gooseberries
Currants
Strawberries
Raspberries

Digitalis 'Saltwood Summer'

Bumblebees are often used in glasshouses to pollinate plants, as they happily stay inside, whereas honeybees keep trying to escape. Bumblebee queens can be kept in hibernation – using a high concentration of carbon dioxide – and reawakened and introduced when a crop is ready to be pollinated. This is very useful commercially.

Favourite bumblebee plants in my garden

Spring:

Comfrey (*Symphytum*)

Pulmonaria

Lenten rose (*Helleborus* × *hybridus*)

Lamiums

Summer:

Sage (*Salvia officinalis*)

Thyme (*Thymus*)

Lavender (*Lavandula*)

Marjoram (*Origanum vulgare*)

Rosemary (*Rosmarinus officinalis*)

Foxglove (*Digitalis*)

Blue cornflower (*Centaurea cyanus*)

Buddleja

Sweet pea (*Lathyrus odorata*)

Lesser scabious (*Scabiosa columbaria*)

Bumblebee facts

Bumblebees are social creatures and live in colonies. They are found in cooler temperate regions and two species live within the Arctic Circle. There are 254 British species of bee, but most are solitary; 25 per cent are on the list of endangered species. Of the 24 British species of bumblebee, 5 are on the list of endangered species. They have been hit badly by the loss of hedgerows and by intensive farming methods – so gardeners should do all they can to provide food and nesting sites. Hedges, compost heaps, leaf litter and old dry stone walls all make good nesting sites; or you can buy artificial sites.

Symphytum orientale

The most common bumblebee species

The first three species below like to nest in old mouse nests. The last three species like to nest in leaf litter or in grassy tussocks.

Buff-tailed bumblebee (*Bombus terrestris*)
Common white-tailed bumblebee (*Bombus lucorum*)
Common red-tailed bumblebee (*Bombus lapidarius*)
Early bumblebee (*Bombus pratorum*)
Common pasture bumblebee (*Bombus pascuorum*)
Common garden bumblebee (*Bombus hortorum*)

CHAPTER THREE

Under the Canopy

The latter half of winter is often colder than the first and it's a good time to learn about your plot, however small it is. You'll be able to see now where the frost hollows are – usually the lowest places. These will be the last to thaw, staying white for longest. A frost hollow indicates that this area will be better for summer- or autumn-flowering plants than for spring flowerers. These cold spots are not suitable for fruit (particularly gooseberries) either, as the flowers or blossom are likely to be frosted. In any case all fruit needs to be grown in the warmer, sunnier areas of the garden as that's where bees, who will pollinate them, prefer to work.

You will also be able to see which areas catch the early morning sunshine. Though such places may seem sheltered and plant-friendly, they are stressful for most plants. Frost can freeze a plant's sap, and sap (just like water) expands on freezing, rupturing the plant's cells. When the sap thaws the plant suffers the full effect of the damage. Even plants that produce their own 'anti-freeze' are vulnerable to sudden thaw. The process is much more devastating when the thaw is rapid – as it will be when the morning sun melts the frost in seconds. Place leafy plants such as box, ivy and hardy ferns here, as their tough leaves are capable of withstanding sudden thaw. The place where the afternoon sun shines during winter and spring will be the warmest spot in the garden at this time of the year – for there is more heat in the rays of afternoon sun. Here is the perfect place for a spring garden.

The area that catches every ray of midday sunshine throughout the year will be the hottest, driest part of the garden. This area will make a silver-leaved summer garden full of lavender, thyme, origanum, dianthus and sage – but only if you leave the site open and don't plant any overhanging trees or shrubs.

As you look round the garden during late winter you will also see some damp, shady places – in the lee of fences or the house – which take most of

Galanthus 'James Backhouse' (growing at Colesbourne Park, near Cirencester, Gloucestershire)

the year to dry out. Dank and miserable they may seem to us, but ferns, thalictrums and bog primulas will love the cool, damp shade. You can utilize the boundaries and edges of your garden by planting hedges, creating an area for hedge-bottom plants – campions, aquilegias and ferns.

The part of the garden that gets the evening sunshine during midsummer will make a pleasant place to sit – the gin terrace so many gardeners need after a hard day. It will also warm up late in the year, as the sun only sets in the north-west when the days are long. Here you could plant an autumn border – one that will get away late and stay late. Consider incorporating some blue plants within view of your gin terrace and seat – pots of agapanthus or blue salvias perhaps – as they will glow like evening stars in the gloaming.

Analysing your garden may take several months or even a year, and of course other factors will also affect your gardening decisions – slopes, views and vistas; getting to know your soil is important too. But if you can make some intelligent deductions in this way you will begin to see plants as living personalities with particular needs which must be accommodated when you plant them in your garden, and not equate choosing a plant with picking an inanimate object like a new settee. Once you have drawn some conclusions about your garden, you will be able to create some seasonal areas of focus – like those Christmas tree lights that glow on one part of the tree after another.

Experienced gardeners know that seasonal borders change through the year and have a peak of perfection that lasts for three months or so before fading. In a natural garden, we accept this waxing and waning as part of the process and find ways to extend the interest. A good device in summer and autumn borders is to leave pockets for colourful old-fashioned bedding plants – but not in the alternating lobelia and alyssum style of bedding. In spring these pockets could contain a medley of yellow tulips, orange wallflowers and blue forget-me-nots. As these fade, you could replant these areas with red dahlias, *Verbena bonariensis* and tender salvias (such as 'Blue Indigo'). You could also use some large containers to draw the eye to a colourful diversion and give the surrounding area a boost. These pockets should be visible from paths, lawns or vistas. Maintaining structure and form in the winter months is another way of extending interest.

The very act of planting for all the seasons and growing a wide range of plants in the places where they do best will increase plant diversity, which in turn will pull in a greater amount of wildlife – adding to your garden's living jigsaw.

The early-spring spotlight

As winter turns into spring, the first part of the garden to shine under the spotlight should be the area that gets the afternoon sunshine at this time of the year. If you're lucky enough to be starting afresh with a naked plot, create your own woodland shade by planting a deciduous tree – preferably fruiting. This will give you shelter and allow early sunshine through the branches. Then add some spring- or winter-flowering shrubs. The layered planting of one tree, some shrubs and some low-level plants will attract more insects and small animal life than an area which relies solely on trees, or just shrubs, or all low-level planting. A spring border is particularly suitable for this multi-layered style of planting. Many spring-flowering plants are natural woodlanders and in a spring border they appreciate a planting that emulates their natural home.

The tree you choose will obviously grow and spread and as it does it will filter and screen your plants from full sun during summer (when its leaves are full out) and expose the plants at ground level to the sky during late autumn and winter. These are perfect conditions for woodlanders and many early bulbs. The tree will have a benevolent effect on its surroundings. The branches will provide shelter from above – keeping the worst of the cold weather away. The tree's root system will provide warmth and drainage – keeping the soil warmer and drier than it would be otherwise. Fruit trees are highly desirable for attracting wildlife. The following ornamental trees will make good individual specimens and also attract wildlife:

Ornamental trees for small gardens

Medlar (*Mespilus germanica*) – a wide tree that produces large white flowers in May, brown fruits in autumn and good autumn colour.

Spindle trees (*Euonymus*) – though technically trees, these are quite shrubby but the following would all be good choices. *E. alatus* is a corky-barked spindle with brilliant crimson-pink leaves in September and shocking two-tone spindle berries. *E. planipes* forms an urn-shaped bush and has large winged fruits. *E. latifolius* also has large fruits with sharp-edged wings.

Malus × *robusta* 'Red Sentinel' – this crab apple has white flowers in the spring and deep red fruits which last all winter.

Oriental hellebore hybrid and *Cardamine quinquefolia*

Winter aconite (*Eranthis hyemalis*)

Decorative hawthorns – *Crataegus persimilis* 'Prunifolia' has white flowers with red anthers and produces lots of fruits which turn from dark green to glossy red. The slim trunk produces a broad-headed tree which colours well in autumn. *C. laevigata* 'Crimson Cloud' has downy grey leaves and red flowers with white centres followed by orange haws.

Sargent's rowan (*Sorbus sargentiana*) has enormous sticky buds in winter, which burst open to reveal slender leaflets. In autumn this small, slow-growing tree has rich red foliage and good-sized clusters of small orange-scarlet fruits. The autumn-flowering cherry *Prunus* × *subhirtella* 'Autumnalis' has early-winter wands of spidery bare branches with a profusion of semi-double white flowers. Reminiscent of snowflakes, these cheer the coldest winter day. Buyer beware, though: this can make a substantial tree.

You can cleverly manage your spring- and winter-flowering shrubs using a technique I first saw in Sue Ward's garden in Eastleigh, Hampshire (open under the National Gardens Scheme). Once your deciduous shrubs (such as viburnums, philadelphus and cotinus) have been growing happily for a couple of years, you can safely remove the lower branches leaving a trunk (or main stem) reaching 2 feet (60 cm) in height. This needs to be done during late spring – when the newly rising sap will seal the wounds as you lop. Once the skirts are lifted you can plant this area right up to the trunk. This allows you to pack more plants into the border – a huge help when you only have a small garden.

The earliest flower at ground level is often the winter aconite (*Eranthis hyemalis*), just pipping the snowdrop to the winning post. The very name bridges the two seasons: *eranthis* means spring-flowering and *hyemalis* means flowering in winter. The bright yellow globes, surrounded by a ruff of green, need a sheltered spot somewhere warm, as the flowers fail to open if the temperature stays below 10°C (50°F). Persuading them to open is vital, as they spread by setting seed and the first bees must find the petals open if they're to be pollinated. South-facing winter troughs or borders against sun-baked walls (even at the bare bases of shrubs) will give them the temperature boost they need on sun-kissed winter days.

The three most useful nectar plants in my spring or woodland border are pulmonarias, hellebores and snowdrops. These underpin the border from February until the first week of May and I use them in abundance. The snowdrops flower first. I have a collection of fifty or so – although that amount is mundane compared to others. The most common species of snowdrop, *Galanthus nivalis*, is the best starting point for budding galanthophiles – it's inexpensive, easy to buy and simple to grow. Start your collection in early spring when many papers and magazines advertise snowdrops 'in the green'. These are raised commercially in fields – usually in Lincolnshire or Norfolk – and are dispatched in March or April when still in leaf.

There are two common sorts: the single, *G. nivalis*, and the double, *G.n.* 'Flore Pleno'. Generally, the doubles clump up more quickly and thickly than the single forms – but they can be clumsy and less elegant. The singles are more stylish to my eye, but in my experience often slower to spread. When your leafy bulbs arrive (in March or April) they will be shrivelled, as they will have just finished flowering. Prepare the soil by digging it thoroughly and adding some organic material and a sprinkling of bonemeal. Separate each bulb and then plant them randomly in clumps of three or five. Mulch them in September with well-rotted organic matter. Repeat the dividing routine every third year and your garden will soon be well stocked.

These two sorts of our possibly native galanthus make tiny bulbs – less than ½ inch (1 cm) in diameter. When dry bulbs are sold in September, they have usually shrivelled in size and they simply don't grow. However, should you spot some large, solid bulbs in September these would be a good investment – but generally, it's better to buy them 'in the green'.

Top The marbled leaves of *Cyclamen hederifolium*, snowdrops and *Cyclamen coum*
Centre *Galanthus* 'Desdemona', one of the Greatorex doubles
Bottom *G. elwesii* 'Comet'

Leaf litter from hazel mimics the woodland floor perfectly and provides all-important shelter.

Once you've succeeded with your first snowdrops, extend your range to include the early, handsome, glaucous-leaved G. elwesii, exposing it to some sunshine at the edge of the spring border. This sturdy, upright snowdrop is very boldly marked with thick dark green. Grow the alluring G.e. var. elwesii 'Magnet', a mid-season single with a bright-white flower held on a curving flower stalk (or pedicel). It trembles and dances. Another strong performer, G. plicatus 'Wendy's Gold', is a plicate (or pleated-leaved) snowdrop and the most robust yellow-marked snowdrop.

The easiest of the readily available doubles are G. nivalis f. pleniflorus 'Pusey Green Tip', G. 'Hill Poë', G. 'Barbara's Double' and G. nivalis 'Blewbury Tart'. All bulk up well. Add some giants too, such as 'Brenda Troyle', 'S. Arnott' and 'Ginns', and you'll have a range of snowdrops that will flower over several weeks.

Hellebores are the perfect partners for snowdrops as they begin to flower in January and continue until late April. This is because hellebores, members of the Ranunculaceae or buttercup family, have an unusual flower structure. The outer part of the flower is made from tough sepals rather than soft petals, which create durable and weather-resistant flowers. (The winter aconite shares the same structure.) Its long-lasting floral presence, combined with handsome foliage, makes it an ideal garden plant. When they first flower, the single-flowered forms contain nectaries which are highly attractive to the first bees. As the flower ages, the nectaries drop off.

The weather-resistant hellebore is a winter beauty, whether plain or spotted.

Your garden centre or nursery will sell several hybrids and species. The best garden performers are listed under *Helleborus × hybridus* – a plant formed by crossing several variable species. These Lenten roses have plain glossy leaves, they are compact (that is, they do not sprawl) and the flowers come in shades varying from white to yellow, apricot to pink and from light rose to deepest slate black. Within this wide colour range there are many variations – pristine single colours, spots, streaks, semi-doubles, circular singles and ragged star shapes. The choice is yours – but the range is so immense that it's important to buy your hellebores when they're flowering.

Helleborus × hybridus is mostly seed-raised and there are some fine strains available – Ashwood and Harvington spring to mind.

Though expensive, these long-lived beauties (which may last for forty years) can be left undivided for many years. I have several stars in my collection and I always remove the seedheads, in order to keep the vigour in the main plant. Whether or not you do this is a matter of preference. Two points are well worth remembering. Should you collect the seed, you should sow it immediately. Secondly, should you wish to divide your hellebores after flowering, take some small 'noses' from the main plant and leave the bulk of the plant undisturbed. Divisions won't grow from old or damaged tissue – which is why the nursery trade has to raise them from seed. Whole hellebores transplant readily, but dividing them can be a tricky process which can lead to disaster – even loss!

Hellebores are greedy feeders and need to be fed heavily twice a year – after flowering and again in September. The feed can be an organic fertilizer (pelleted chicken manure or 6X) or a mulch of garden compost or manure.

Though hellebores are easy garden plants, there are two problems you should be aware of. The leaves can be attacked by aphids – though in a well-stocked, natural garden the aphids will soon disappear. Hellebores also succumb to a black spot disease called *Coniothyrium hellebori* if they're under stress when they're growing, so feed your plants well. As we suffer wetter, milder winters this disease is becoming more prevalent. Remove any leaves that develop the telltale black marks as soon as you see them. If these touch the ground, the spores will be transferred from the leaf to the soil on splashes of rain – the way all black spot diseases and many other fungal diseases are spread. These infected leaves should be burnt or taken out of the garden, not placed on the compost heap. Mulch the plants well to create a barrier between soil and leaf.

One of the best ways to avoid any fungal disease in any plant is to ensure that there is always a flow of air round the plant. For healthy hellebores, follow this regime. Give the crowns of the plant a good tidy in late September before the autumn rains, removing any large leaves that are lying prone against the soil. Then, close to Christmas, remove all the leaves. This sounds harsh, but when your hellebores come into flower, in the weeks after Christmas, each stem will have a fresh ruff of

Top Plum-coloured hellebore, its nectaries clearly visible
Bottom White hellebore

new leaves round the buds. When you remove the leaves you also take away the hiding place of mice, and they can devour the new buds.

When planting newly acquired hellebores, take them out of the pot and remove the top inch of soil from the plant. Place this at the bottom of the hole. Plant the new hellebore and replace the missing top inch of compost with garden soil. This will help to prevent the fungal diseases brought in from the nursery. Indeed this is a good tip for any newly bought plant – you will never get bittercress in your borders if you follow this system. Nursery hellebores are regularly sprayed against the black spot disease, so the plants look healthy when you buy them, but spores will lurk in that top inch of soil.

When visiting nurseries, you will see some other hellebore hybrids and species, but they do not perform as well in the garden as the *H. × hybridus* selections. The Christmas rose (*H. niger*) is a miffy beast in the open border, producing but a few muddy flowers, and it is best grown in a raised bed, against a very sheltered wall or – much easier – in a pot. Some hellebore species are less than hardy – *H. lividus,* for instance. Another, *H. argutifolius,* is only worth growing in a large woodland garden, for within two years every stem of its apple-green flowers will have spread across the ground like the spokes on a large wagon wheel, flopping over everything else. There is a silver-leaved cultivar called 'Silver Lace' which looks stunning in a container, but I haven't grown it in the open garden. *H. foetidus,* a sun-loving native hellebore with clusters of small green bells, edged in red,

Top *Helleborus argutifolius*
Bottom A choice unnamed pulmonaria

is another candidate for a large woodland garden. *H. lividus* and *H. × sternii* (the latter a cross between *H. argutifolius* and *H. lividus*) hate hard weather and are short-lived in the garden.

The pulmonarias rank just as highly as the hellebores in my esteem. Their flowers are usually slightly later and take over from the hellebore as the chief nectar provider. Most pulmonarias have spotted or silvered leaves and these dappled patterns, said to resemble a diseased lung, have given the plant the common name of lungwort. The earliest to flower is a tomato-red pulmonaria with plain, unspotted leaves – *P. rubra*. This makes a large, spreading clump and is not suitable for smaller gardens, though it makes great show when planted with *Helleborus argutifolius*. A variegated cream and green form named *P. rubra* 'David Ward' (after Beth Chatto's propagator) is a much more restrained plant. This needs shelter from the sun and wind to avoid turning to a brown crisp, but it's well worth growing tucked into deep shade.

Pulmonarias produce clusters of flowers, many of which open pink and then change to blue. This two-tone blend gives the plant the common name of soldiers and sailors (after old-fashioned red soldiers and blue sailors). The flowers are highly popular with bees and cross readily. Consequently there are countless named pulmonarias. I like to deadhead my plants, as I want to preserve my named varieties and not raise chance seedlings – but again whether or not you do this is a matter of preference. I remove each cluster of flowers just before it fades.

Of the hundred or so named pulmonarias for sale, there are a few 'greats' that deserve mentioning. For spotted leaves and brick-pink flowers, *P. saccharata* 'Leopard' cannot be beaten in the garden. While the spots in other pulmonarias merge and fudge together, 'Leopard's distinct square spots never change and it always looks clean and neat. *P.* Opal, also known as 'Ocupol', has good spotted leaves and pale blue flowers and grows strongly – something most of the pale-flowered forms don't achieve. White pulmonarias, though very fresh and pure, are very restrained growers.

P. 'Majesté', which has warm pink-magenta flowers, is the best silver-leaved pulmonaria,

even providing a silver presence during the winter months – which is a rarity, as most pulmonaria leaves are silver only during the summer. P. 'Diana Clare' has violet-blue flowers and pale green-silver leaves which are the colour of well-weathered copper roofs, even in winter. 'Trevi Fountain' is a deep cobalt blue with long spotted leaves. P. 'Roy Davidson' is a dainty, fairly late, Wedgwood blue – a diminutive fellow. P. saccharata 'Dora Bielefeld' has spotted leaves and pale pink flowers in abundance. P. 'Victorian Brooch' is a round-leaved magenta and P. longifolia 'Ankum' is a late-flowering blue with narrow spotted leaves.

Most of the pulmonarias I grow have good foliage. I want this to endure through the summer months, when they make a real contribution to the fading woodland border. If I left the leaves intact throughout the summer, they would almost certainly succumb to mildew and end up looking very unattractive. So, by mid-May I have cut back all my pulmonarias to within an inch of their lives. For this short back

and sides I use a single-handed shear – a much easier thing to brandish than two-handed shears. I immediately sprinkle a light dressing of blood, fish and bone on the soil around each plant and then carefully water each plant well with a gallon of water enhanced with comfrey tea (see below). This gives them a nitrogen-rich boost, promoting strong new leaves. If mildew – a disease exacerbated by dry conditions – strikes, I repeat the haircut.

One group of pulmonarias I have failed to succeed with are the plain-leaved angustifolia types. These have desirable gentian-blue flowers in late spring. 'Blue Ensign' is the best known, but it struggles in my dry garden. These types disappear underground during summer and re-emerge the following spring and never seem to get going here. You may be luckier.

On the outer edges of the woodland border I have planted a close relative of the pulmonaria – the comfrey. The three comfreys I have chosen are upright, rather than spreading. Symphytum caucasicum is a bright blue with a greyish-green leaf; S. orientale has pure white

Above from left *Pulmonaria* 'Lewis Palmer'; *P. rubra*; *P. Opal*; *P. saccharata* 'Dora Bielefeld'

A wild colony of our native *Anemone nemorosa*

flowers against fresh-green leaves; and S. 'Rubrum' has wine-red flowers and mid-green leaves. Comfrey is useful for two reasons. Firstly it remains in leaf (as a rosette) for ten months of the year, adding shelter and leafy interest. Secondly the flower's cyme unfurls and provides a series of insect-attracting flowers over many weeks, bridging spring and summer. The substantial leaves make a nitrogen-rich plant food. I place 2–3 inches (5–7 cm) of chopped-up leaves in the bottom of a bucket, fill the bucket with water and leave it for a few weeks. When using the mixture, I dilute it – roughly 1 pint (0.5 litres) comfrey mixture to 2 gallons (9 litres) of water. It also makes a compost accelerator, when chopped and added to the heap. Its drawback –

and there's always one, isn't there? – is a tendency to produce unwanted stubborn seedlings which can (and do) root anywhere.

Spring border fillers

You can fit any of the following well-behaved plants between hellebores, pulmonarias and snowdrops to provide more flowers without any fear of their romping through the border:

Wood anemone (*Anemone nemorosa*) – a gentle native plant, the best cultivars of which are the double white 'Vestal', the green-centred (but slow) 'Green Fingers', the mid-blue 'Robinsoniana' and the green 'aberration' 'Virescens', which is a froth of divided leaf and has no flowers.

The early-flowering *Cardamine quinquefolia*

Anemone ranunculoides – a yellow anemone that also behaves well here. I grow the pale lemon *A.* × *lipsiensis* 'Pallida', a hybrid between it and the wood anemone. Don't confuse these woodlanders with *A. blanda*, a plant that likes the sun and adores being grown in containers.

Bleeding hearts (*Dicentra*) provide ferny foliage and locket-shaped flowers from April onwards in perfectly balanced measures. I avoid the showy *D. spectabilis,* which collapses at the first touch of frost, and the glaucous-leaved forms, which jar in a woodland setting. My two enduring favourites are the clean white *D. eximia* 'Snowdrift' and the deep red *D.* 'Bacchanal'.

Cardamine quinquefolia is a useful plant – a spreading lady's smock which sends up dark green leaves in January and mauve flowers by February before conveniently disappearing beneath the ground.

Lesser celandines (*Ranunculus ficaria*) are February buttercups – just as lacquered and high-gloss as the summer meadow flowers. They were Wordsworth's favourite flower, celebrated by his cronky rhyme 'Little Flower! – I'll make a stir, / Like a great astronomer …' It never caught on as his 'host of golden daffodils' poem did. Poor Wordsworth decreed that this humble flower should grace his tombstone, but the mason reproduced the greater celandine instead. There are red-leaved forms such as 'Brazen Hussy' but most have marbled leaves. 'Randall's White', 'Double Mud' (a cream) and 'Coppernob' (orange) are just three of about 120 listed.

THE GROUND BEETLE

Whenever I'm using my trowel in the garden, or I move a container or piece of stone, I'm almost certain to see a shiny beetle scurrying away. These are ground beetles. During the day they shelter somewhere cool and dark, but at night they spend their time searching for small slugs, caterpillars and insects; they also eat slug eggs, grubs and insect eggs. So we need them in our gardens.

They are called ground beetles because they live at and below the soil surface. In the winter months they shelter in moss, leaf litter or amid garden debris, so it's important to leave some undisturbed areas during winter and spring. Some beetles are garden pests (the vine weevil and the Colorado beetle, for instance), but generally ground beetles are good insects – devouring many pests at soil level. They are specially adapted for hunting, having powerful mouth parts and long legs. Once they've located their prey with the aid of their sensitive antennae, they rush towards it and seize it between their powerful mandibles. There is no escape.

Ground beetles thrive under a leaf canopy and sparsely planted gardens will not have large numbers of beetles. Plant densely and lay large sections of tree trunk at the back of the border to provide shelter.

THE VINE WEEVIL

Weevils are a specialized form of beetle with mouth parts adapted to penetrate plant tissue. My garden is rarely troubled by vine weevil – I think the ground beetles soon sniff out the grubs. They can be devastating. Each adult vine weevil looks like a large beetle with a yellow-speckled ridged body. They cannot fly, but are most active in the evening and live for three months and lay 300–600 eggs over the summer. Here is a working regime for getting rid of these devastating pests:

- Always use a gritty, soil-based compost when containerizing plants. Avoid soft peaty composts.
- Certain plants with fleshy roots are very prone to vine weevils – heucheras, sedums and primroses (*Primula*), saxifrages and epimediums. If you are growing them in a pot, surround the surface of the soil with sharp Cornish grit to deter adult vine weevils from laying their eggs.

Vine weevil

- The adults climb, they can't fly and they are active at night. They often climb towards light, so leaving an outside light on after nightfall is a good way of luring them towards it. Check the wall every evening and kill any you find.
- If possible, never overwinter pots of plants because vine weevil can survive in very low temperatures. Take cuttings and start again wherever possible.
- If you have containers of plants that must be kept over winter, when spring arrives, remove each plant from the pot (by gently gripping the stem) and look for any telltale gaps in the root system. If there are gaps, look for any white grubs and destroy them. Shake off as much soil as possible, wash the roots and repot. Then treat with nematodes. If your plant feels insecure when you grip it, and comes away with little root, you may have an infested plant.
- Using nematodes (available from the Green Gardener, 01603 715096, www.greengardener.co.uk) in spring and autumn, though expensive, works as long as the soil is moist and the weather is warm – over 12°C (53°F).
- Hedgehogs, moles, birds, frogs and toads, and especially ground beetles, devour the grubs and the adults.

SPRING

CHAPTER FOUR

Swathes of Grass

THINK ABOUT YOUR LAWN CREATIVELY, ALTERING THE LENGTH
AND THE MOWING REGIMES TO CREATE AESTHETICALLY
PLEASING AREAS OF LONGER GRASS THAT ARE
ATTRACTIVE TO WILDLIFE

In my days as a student teacher, encouraged by my bullying tutor I organized a project based around mini-beasts for the first half of the summer term. I took a class of bubbly eight-year-olds outside, with plastic pots, lenses and old sheets to lay under trees. The task was to scour the school playground and flower beds, and try to discover some interesting insect life. Forty sharp-eyed children took part in the hunt on a sunny May day, hoping to draw, study and sketch.

Hours of searching and shaking revealed only a few aphids and some woodlice – not enough for a project. We were disappointed, but it was a typical inner-city school in Birmingham and, in those days when local authorities still employed groundsmen, a team arrived every week or so to mow, tidy and spray; and when I looked at the scalped grass, the strimmed edges and the patches of sprayed weeds on the outer edges I had to concede that if I were an insect I would be forced by the lack of shelter and food to move next door.

Years later, after the memory of that disappointment had faded, I repeated the project – this time taking an equally bubbly mix of children to a churchyard. Though the churchyard was in the centre of Daventry, it was knee high in cow parsley and long grass, and it was at that moment in the year when summer breathes on you. Using the same equipment that we'd had in Birmingham, we found that the whole area was flecked with moving insects catching the sunlight. Hoverflies, bees and flies milled around. Beetles scurried and birdlife abounded. Being careful not to flatten the grass, we watched them, lost in wonder at the busy movement. We came back with enough material for a two-week blast of activity – and went back for more. I would like to think that the school in Birmingham could have been like this too, given the chance.

Previous page *Crocus chrysanthus* 'Cream Beauty'
Left Mixed crocus planted in lawns during September will provide early nectar for any bees.

Natural gardens can have elements of these two extremes within them. You can carefully maintain your garden in some areas, but give other areas the freedom to develop. There are several possible strategies. Some gardeners meticulously mow the main part of the lawn, edge the borders carefully and manicure the first two feet of the flower borders (closest to the lawn edge) very thoroughly. Visitors observe the neatness at the most visible points and fail to notice the less-manicured depths beyond. Others maintain all the borders and lawn and leave the outer edges of the garden – the boundaries – to their own devices, and doing this doesn't make the garden look neglected. These unkempt areas of either strategy still need managing. You should remove seedheads from invasive plants (dandelions and thistles), and pernicious weeds (such as ground elder) need to be constantly worried or contained by a wide strip of mowed grass. But the unmanicured areas add plant diversity and provide shelter.

The lawn – the perfect opportunity

Most gardeners have a lawn and many aspire to perfect bowling-green stripes. Frighteningly, 80 per cent of all the garden chemicals bought are applied to lawns. Even worm casts are seen as a problem by some gardeners. I have never used a chemical on my lawn, and I haven't done much scarifying and aerating, although these two physical activities can do much to improve the lawn – and your waistline. There is a new sort of lawn mower (in use at the HDRA's Yalding Garden in Kent) that pushes the clippings down into the lawn, negating the need for expensive chemical feeds. The natural gardener must adopt a chemical-free regime with the lawn – the rich green highly fed sward is not for us.

It's also the perfect opportunity to combine the manicured and the wilder styles, using them side by side. It's possible to have some parts short and tidy and leave others to grow. Long grass may look ragged on its own, but when paths are cut through the swathe, or the longer grass is surrounded by neat lawn, the garden takes on a smarter look. This device, used in many National Trust gardens to great effect, allows wildflowers and swaying grass to shelter and sustain our wildlife, and looks much more attractive than expanses of closely mown grass. Some butterflies – the skipper and the brown families – lay their eggs on tall native grasses and although these will not be found in lawn seed mixtures, some native grass seeds may well be in the seed bank lying in the soil. Crested dog's-tail (*Cynosurus cristatus*), meadow-grass (*Poa annua*) and sweet vernal grass (*Anthoxanthum odoratum*) come up in my bulb lawns.

The message is: look at your lawn with a more creative eye and use your mower to create swards of long grass – close to shrubs, round trees, in the middle of the lawn and on the garden edges. Have some fun and be less stereotyped.

Flowers for longer grass

Once longer areas of grass are established, the easiest way to influence the flowering plants within them is to alter the mowing regime. Encourage the plants you want – ox-eye daisies (*Leucanthemum vulgare*), campion (*Silene dioica*), cow parsley (*Anthriscus sylvestris*) and wild orchids – by mowing after they have set

Long grass surrounded by neat lawn offers shelter, but still looks cared for.

seed, which is usually in mid-August. Religiously remove by hand the plants you don't want – thistles, buttercups and nettles.

Prince Charles, in his Highgrove garden, has introduced wildflowers into the meadows by using plug plants. It is difficult to introduce these plants, grown in a nursery in small plastic cells so that they can be inserted into grass, in the small garden, as they (wild flowers such as cowslips (*Primula veris*), cornflowers (*Centaurea cyanus*), yellow rattle (*Rhinanthus*), poppies (*Papaver*) and corn marigolds (*Xanthophthalmum segetum*) can soon be overrun by coarse grasses. The run-off from arable fields (where nitrogen fertilizers are used) is affecting many naturally run meadows, as demonstrated by the flourishing coarse grasses and nettles close to rivers (on the banks of the Evenlode, for instance). On farmed grazing land and in larger estate-sized gardens, sheep can be used to crop the grass, which encourages the flowers and finer grasses. The key to success is to keep the soil fertility low, by removing all grass clippings and not fertilizing. Low fertility discourages coarse lush grasses. Finally, make sure that any mowing happens after the plug plants have set seed – late August or September.

Certain plants can survive and compete in rough grass. We see these toughies on the sides of the roads, thriving despite the nitrogen-rich outpourings of our car exhausts. Bladder campion (*Silene vulgaris*), common agrimony (*Agrimonia eupatoria*), cow parsley (*Anthriscus sylvestris*), field scabious (*Knautia arvensis*), greater knapweed (*Centaurea scabiosa*), lesser knapweed (*Centaurea nigra*), meadow cranesbill (*Geranium pratense*) and musk mallow (*Malva moschata*) are all toughies that can compete in grass. You can introduce them by sprinkling seeds on freshly cleared soil, having first rotavated the site. The flowers look pretty and are important nectar sources as well.

This rake-and-sow process is taking place on newly built roadsides throughout the country, but some of the seed mixtures used (bought in from abroad) are introducing some strange plants – California poppy (*Eschscholzia californica*), for instance, can be spotted on Gloucester roadside verges. So if you are using seed mixtures, study them carefully before ordering. Make sure that you buy meadow mixtures, not, for instance, prairie mixtures. Distributing your own seeds, collected from nursery-grown plants, is another alternative. The mowing regime that encourages these toughies involves a late, high-blade April cut, followed by a second low-blade late-August or September cut. Again the key to success is to keep the fertility as low as possible. That means no fertilizers.

If this approach seriously interests you, research the project by looking at the local flora on untrimmed roadside verges or meadowland close to your home – as different areas of the country vary. The charity Flora-for-Fauna can supply you with a list of native species suitable for your area, many of which could do well planted in grass. Visit its website, which is hosted by the Natural History Museum (http: www.naturalhistorymuseum.org.uk), and put in your postcode for an extensive printout. Note, though, that some plants (such as the poppy and the foxglove) need regular soil disturbance to flower and these are conditions not easily met within grassy areas.

The bulb lawn

You can also use unmown grassy areas to create bulb lawns. These are easy to establish, and perform within six months. I have two such areas, one under the outer edges of the apple tree and the other close to the contorted hazel; they contain crocuses, miniature narcissus and snake's head fritillaries. This trouble-free, long-lasting trio give colour from February until the end of April and by then some of the toughies – bladder campion etc. – may well take over. If you combine toughies and bulbs, restrict the mow to a once a year, late-August scalping.

Start your bulb lawn by planting daffodils (*Narcissus*) and crocus bulbs during September.

Garden narcissi are very diverse – many are hybrids from several species. Generally speaking, the yellow and orange daffodils flower earlier than the creams and whites. In my garden I've chosen vigorous daffodils with simple shapes, which give me March flowers, and they are all yellow varieties or species. I favour the shorter, smaller narcissi for two reasons. Firstly, they give a sense of scale to smaller lawns and gardens and, secondly, they stand up to late-spring weather (which can include snow). They are much more resilient than the taller, willowier daffodils. I remove the faded flowers and divide the bulbs, in June usually, every fifth year.

Jaunty yellows

Narcissus 'Jetfire' has swept-back yellow petals (reflecting its *N. cyclamineus* blood) and a red-orange trumpet and is the best daffodil I grow – a bright spring spark.

N. 'Tête-à-tête' – when truly happy this produces double heads of yellow flowers, but it is a resilient, compact performer in grass.

N. 'February Gold' – an early low-growing yellow with a darker yellow cup.

Paler delicacies

The wild forms of daffodil have a delicate, fragile look about them that suits a natural garden. Both of these are commercially available:

Tenby daffodil (*Narcissus obvallaris*) – this long-lasting daffodil (possibly native to Wales) has yellow outers and a yellow trumpet.

Lent lily (*N. pseudonarcissus*) has two-tone flowers – pale yellow outers and a darker yellow trumpet. This native grows close to Gloucester, in Herefordshire, on the Welsh borders, in the Lake District and in Yorkshire.

Crocuses

Crocuses enjoy sunny, well-drained sites, preferring sunny gravel screes and tend to peter out in lawns. I plant some crocuses every year. They flower in February and attract early bees. I choose small crocuses such as *C. chrysanthus*

Top *Narcissus* 'Jetfire', ring-fenced with crossed sticks
Centre *N.* 'February Gold'
Bottom *N. pseudonarcissus*

I favour small, dainty crocuses.

punch its way through the grass without lifting the whole piece of turf. Daffodils need to be planted in September as they have a long growing season. They produce their flowering shoots by Christmas and the fully formed buds lurk just under the soil surface, waiting for warmer weather to arrive. They also emerge through the same hole year after year.

In order to mark the bulbs and separate them from the main lawn, I add a decorative border of crossed hazel sticks. This is an idea I copied from a Worcestershire garden. In January or early February I cut 15-inch (35-cm) lengths of pencil-thick hazel branches from the edges of the garden and overlap them in the form of Xs to create a definite edge to the oval in which I have planted the bulbs.

When I give the lawn the first mow of the year (round the bulb lawn and not over it), which is often in March, I cut as close to the sticks as possible and the whole area looks managed and kempt. The long grass within the criss-cross sticks creates another habitat for insects and small mammals.

The two practical benefits of a criss-cross hazel boundary are that mowers that rely on electric cables have something to engage before they slice across the fragile bulb stems and guillotine the buds or flowers. Secondly, the bulbs are ring-fenced against clumsy feet – including your own.

Snake's head fritillaries (*Fritillaria meleagris*) are better established as potted plants and then transplanted in flower as these are easier to get going in long grass than dry bulbs planted in

'Cream Beauty', 'Blue Pearl', 'Snow Bunting' and 'Goldilocks'. I also grow *C. sieberi* 'Violet Queen' because I hate the over-large exuberant Dutch giants: they remind me of punctured, helpless balloons, whereas the small species types are flickering flames. I also fight shy of the self-seeding *C. tommasinianus* types of crocus, having seen other gardeners struggling to eradicate thousands of them.

The technique for planting bulbs in a lawn is to mark out an oval area and within it lift thin squares of turf with a spade and distress and batter it – pretend it's an adversary – and then, after planting bulbs underneath, reposition each piece. This pounding breaks up the dense root system of the turf and allows each bulb to

Pots of bulbs can be a moveable feast for the eyes. Tulips do well in terracotta containers and can be moved into cool shade if late spring is very warm. This extends their life.

Fritillaria meleagris

should produce tall seedheads. The resulting seedlings take three years to flower.

Both my bulb lawns keep their stick edging until late August and then I remove them (and recycle them on winter fires) to allow a thorough mow or clip. I collect the long grass cuttings after a day or so in the hope that all lurking insects will escape removal with the clippings. Doing this leaves an unsightly yellow thatch for a few days, but the whole area greens up when the September rains arrive.

Grass cuttings tip

Most gardeners use a grass box to collect their cuttings when mowing which they empty on to the compost heap; but too many grass clippings make a sticky, smelly compost. Others place their clippings under shrubs, or round fruit trees as a moisture-retentive mulch; but this green damp mulch looks very unsightly, and mulches made from leafy material decompose, taking nitrogen from the soil below and robbing it of nutrients in the short term. The following technique helps to solve the problem partially. When you mow, take a plastic sheet and lay it on the ground. Place the clippings in a pile on the sheet. Leave these for at least twenty-four hours and then turn them. Leave them again. In warm weather, the clippings decompose quickly and turn a dull brown. You can then add them to the compost heap or use them as a brown mulch. This looks better, although the almost-rotted clippings may still remove some nutrients in the short term.

September. You can choose a mixture of white and deep burgundy fritillaries. My population is slowly increasing as the plants self-seed, and their chequered or tessellated petals are a great addition to my spring garden. *F. meleagris* thrives naturally in water meadows – they can be seen in all their glory on Magdalen College Meadow near the river Thames in Oxford, for instance. Low-lying gardens with a high water table are perfect – but I still manage them here in the highish Cotswolds.

It is worth persevering with snake's head fritillaries, for after your crocuses and daffodils have faded these will take over the baton. They often produce two or three flowers, so extending their flowering season, and then

THE HEDGEHOG

If you hear snuffling and grunting during late spring, you'll know that you've got a hedgehog. Often you will never see your shy garden visitor, but the droppings he leaves from late April onwards, dark and little-finger sized, will indicate his presence. You may get lucky and see him as he begins his evening walk to look for slugs, insects and larvae. At night he will search out any hidden logs at the back of the border and visit the pond for a drink.

I know that my resident hedgehogs (I think I've got at least three) hibernate in three places in the garden – under a wooden shed, to one side of an enormous *Iris unguicularis* and in the beech leaf litter close to the oil tank at the back of the house. They go to the same places every year and I have discovered these sites by chance when sweeping and tidying leaves in spring. This is a job that you should leave until early May, as there may be other hibernators under the hedges. Beech leaf litter accumulates in all three hibernation sites, indicating a need for a dry site with debris, be it leaves or stems.

Hedgehogs are becoming rarer and rarer. They insist on making a long circuit every night and many are killed on the road. They are not slow-moving but they do seem to be drawn to tarmac. Every summer I sit in my study working – with its view down the drive – next to a large cardboard box and a hand shovel. If I spot one heading for the road, I rush out and take it to the furthest depths of the garden. It's my way of trying to save their lives, as well as keep them in my garden. But within a couple of minutes it's ready for escape plan B.

Slug bait has also added to their decline, and the recent weather pattern of on-and-off winters and warm dry springs has really damaged them, as hedgehogs wake early from hibernation and there is little food for them in dry springs. Cat food is a good supplement, but don't give them milk, as it upsets their stomachs. Water is much better. If you have a pond, design it so that the sides are shallow or place a wide plank walkway to the edge. Otherwise your only sighting of a hedgehog in your garden is likely to be of a dead floating one.

CHAPTER FIVE

Water Magic

USE NATIVE PLANTS WHEREVER POSSIBLE, ESPECIALLY NEAR WATER

I'm not going to suggest that all your garden plants should be British natives – that would exclude some stunners such as the hybrid witch hazel, the magnolia and the buddleja. A 'native-only' rule would also exclude from our planting schemes almost all roses, snowdrops and the most garden-worthy hellebores. However, natural gardeners should use as many British natives as they can within their gardens, for these plants are specific food plants for our native insects, butterflies and birds. Their futures depend on these plants. Since one in every eight plants in the world is threatened with extinction, we need to view our gardens – whether they're in urban or rural areas – as important mini-nature reserves, not neat garden rooms. The charity Flora-for-Fauna lists of native species suitable for different areas include plants for both wild and maintained garden areas.

There's another important consideration when choosing between native and alien plants. Native plants have settled and live more or less in harmony with each other in their shared environment. When you plant an alien species it could – despite being perfectly well behaved in its own home environment – become rampant and invasive, eradicating our native plants as it does so. The Japanese knotweed (*Fallopia japonica*), fed by our warm, mild climate, is the example always cited. This weed started life as a garden ornamental and now smothers everything where it grows. It and other similarly invasive alien species could be wiped out by chemical sprays, used again and again, but this technique is undesirable because it kills everything else close by and can't be used when plants grow close to water. Alien plants can (and do) wreak havoc close to watercourses, where areas of damp mud are ripe for colonization. Also alien water plants can grow much faster than our natives.

Water plants like the Australian swamp stonecrop (*Crassula helmsii*), floating pennywort (*Hydrocotyle ranunculoides*) and parrot-feather (*Myriophyllum aquaticum*) are colonizing whole ponds and watercourses – crowding out our native pond plants and providing little benefit to insect and

A small pond is a source of wonder and a refuge for your ground force of toads, newts and frogs.

other animal life. Worse still, many of these alien plants resemble their native counterparts and certain nurseries sell the dangerous alien as the real native, without even realizing. Alien plants can be unknown quantities, and grown in ponds and streams they are mad, bad and dangerous to know. When planting a garden pond, which we want to act as a lure for amphibians, insects and birds, natives are not only desirable but essential.

The magic of the garden pond

Unless you've had a pond, it's hard to convey the sort of excitement it can bring into a garden. During spring and summer a pond is a source of great delight and wonder. At mine, early-spring mornings often start with the mellow sound of croaking toads crooning for a mate. Then there's the excitement of seeing the first toads clasp together and spawn. The straight strands of spawn (very different from the rounded clump that frogs produce) look like A-roads on a map as they weave elaborately through the plants. Gradually, as the water warms, the tadpoles

wriggle free. Just about that time, the first clutch of damsel flies emerge, leaving their split cases on the water plantain leaves.

When the hot weather comes, the fresh, lush greenery surrounding the pond freshens the garden, however dry and tired the rest of it is – one immediately understands why Italianate gardens rely so heavily on water. Then in high summer, clumsy nymphs slowly clamber on to the straight stems of pond plants. These iridescent dragonflies force their way out of their nymph armour and stretch out their wings in the sunshine – and their entrance is a good guarantee of fine weather to come, for they rarely get it wrong. Their immobility can last for a whole day.

The excitement these creatures cause! Different species emerge at different times of the year – and you can watch it all happen. The short stubby darters seem to emerge first here, zigzagging over the garden to return to the same upright stem again and again. Later the slender hawkers fight their way clear of their nymph suit, as if being born. They glide and

Above from left Toad; toads mating in spring; a pair of mating red damselflies; darter dragonfly

skim sedately over the garden – following the same lap over and over. Many migrant dragonfly species arrive through the summer, drawn to the water. At this time of year I fantasize about having a large pond, like the one at Upton House in Warwickshire (a National Trust house). I always manage to squeeze in a visit to Upton, choosing the perfect weather for dragonfly watching.

Having a pond will be a constant fascination and add another dimension to your garden. A pond will entice a greater range of insects and other small animals. It will be visited by birds and hedgehogs, and the insect life which will skate on the surface, hover above and dip into the water will mean that there's always something to see. If the expanse is large enough, it will reflect glimpses of the garden – adding a watery shimmer to the views from seats and house.

The biggest advantage, though, is not the aerial display but the process beneath the water. A pond will provide a home for frogs, toads and newts, and they have a diet partly made up of slugs, the gardener's greatest enemy.

Some considerations
Safety
The biggest consideration when building a pond is one of child safety. If you have children under seven who play in your garden, my advice would be to wait until they reach their teenage years. By then you will often feel like chucking them into cold water and they'll be large enough to clamber out. With young children, the risks of a pond outweigh the benefits as, however often you warn them of danger, they will act unpredictably – especially when you're not looking.

Size
If family safety allows, you want an open expanse of water at least 6 feet (1.8 metres) in length and 36 inches (90 cm) in width – or larger if possible. This will attract your ground force of helpers (frogs, toads and newts).

When
The ideal time to start making a new pond is early September, when landscaping is still possible. The most successful time to introduce new pond plants, though, is spring.

Lythrum salicaria

Dos and Don'ts

Your pond should have gently sloping sides so that hedgehogs, also great devourers of slugs, can drink without drowning. Goldfish are banned because they eat the tadpoles. Fountains are also out during the tadpole season. Water pumps suck them in and mangle them and the disturbance caused by splashing water doesn't suit small tadpoles – how would you like it?. Within the pond there should be two levels. A deep area, approaching 36 inches (90 cm), will provide cover in all weathers and support a different range of plants. A shallow shelf, where the water warms up easily early in the year, will support another group of plants, and the edge of the pond yet another. These three different habitats will widen your range of plants. More diversity means more insect, bird and animal lifelines – yes, I know you've heard it before, but …

Then, they grow away enthusiastically. Few things look as bleak as a newly made pond, but within three months you'll wonder why you didn't make one long ago.

Where

The tendency is to tuck a pond into a corner of the garden, but it's far better to allow yourself enough space to plant all around the pond, so that it merges into the garden setting and you can have different views of it throughout the day. Position it close to an area of long grass to allow frogs and toads some cover, and make sure that the pond isn't close to overhanging trees and their falling leaves, which make the water stagnant.

Critical points in making a pond

- Choose a level site, or create one.
- Mark out the shape with a hose pipe or a rope, choosing a round shape.
- Remove the turf.
- Dig the deepest part of the pond first – up to 36 inches (90 cm).
- Make the shallow shelf in a sunny spot.
- Use a spirit level resting on a large plank to check the sides of the pond. This ensures that the sides are level with each other and that the lining won't show when the pond is full. This is vital to the finished pond, so accuracy will pay dividends. Get the levels wrong and the lines on the higher side will always show.
- Remove any sharp stones from the pond floor.

- Check that the shape of the dug-out area resembles a gentle saucer.
- Choose the best-quality liner – a thick black butyl is best. There are special matting liners to go between the butyl and the soil, but these are expensive. A good cheaper alternative is old newspapers soaked in water. If you have any old pieces of carpet or carpet underlay (though I swore not to mention these), place these on top of the wet newspapers. Or you can use sand.
- Place the lining in the hole and gently anchor the sides and the bottom with old bricks or stone. Then slowly fill the pond with tap water. Waterbutt water is best, but tap water (brought to the pond by hose) is perfectly acceptable and a lot easier.
- Leave everything to settle for a week or so and then trim the liner (leaving at least 12 inches /30 cm round the edge of the pond) and cover the edges with stones, paving or soil.
- Add some sieved soil to the water, to allow plants to establish.

Planting and managing the pond

Plants are needed to oxygenate the water, to provide habitat and to cover the surface of the pond, which prevents algae from forming. Too much sunlight on open water will inevitably produce green algae. Every pond will need time to get the balance right, so if yours gets algae, don't resort to chemicals: just wait and if it remains grow more surface-covering plants such as the fringed water lily. If you get blanket weed, remove it with a cane. Ponds tend to become overgrown and every two or three years clumps of plants will need dividing during the autumn. This means that many gardeners with ponds will be happy to pass on some of their surplus plants.

Caltha palustris

When you go to the garden centre, avoid the showy water lilies and think simple British natives. Here are some well-behaved water plants for small ponds, divided into four groups:

Submerged plants

Hornwort (*Ceratophyllum demersum*) – long, branching fragile stems with whorls of fine, divided leaves. Insignificant flowers.

Ivy-leaved duckweed (*Lemna trisulca*) – pointed lance-shaped, irregularly branched fronds up to ½ inch (1 cm) long. Drifts under water, but rises up to the surface when in flower. Flowers are insignificant.

Whorled water-milfoil (*Myriophyllum spicatum*) – long, submerged stems with finely divided leaves in whorls of four. Spikes, of insignificant flowers, rise up above water in summer.

Seedheads of water plantain and the Japanese iris (*Iris ensata*)

Water soldier

Floating plants

Fringed water lily (*Nymphoides peltata*) – small, circular leaves on long, floating stems. Small yellow flowers with fringed petal edges appear in July and August.

Water soldier (*Stratiotes aloides*) – floating rosettes of spiky green leaves which rise to the surface in warm weather, producing small white flowers in June.

Frog-bit (*Hydrocharis morsus-ranae*) – free-floating, small, round water-lily-like leaves. Graceful, but extensive. Small, white, three-lobed flowers from May until August.

Marginal plants

Water plantain (*Alisma plantago-aquatica*) – upright, large, narrowish leaves form a tight clump. Topped with a mass of tiny white flowers on tall branching stems in July and August reaching 30 inches (80 cm) – spectacular in frost. Flowering rush (*Butomus umbellatus*) – narrow, rush-like leaves about 36 inches (90 cm) and pink umbels of flowers on rigid stems during summer. Arrowhead (*Sagittaria sagittifolia*) – large, glossy

leaves, pointed like an arrowhead. The white flowers come in whorls of three on upright spikes in June and July. It can reach 24 inches (60 cm).

Waterside

Marsh marigold (*Caltha palustris*) – large yellow buttercup flowers in mid-spring and bold, green rounded leaves.

Loosestrife (*Lythrum salicaria*) – tall, blue-pink slender spikes of flowers in midsummer, reaching well over 6 feet (1.8 m). Makes a good winter silhouette – and I like the non-seeding double 'Feuerkereze' (syn. 'Firecandle').

Planting round the pond

I don't grow the traditional moisture-loving ligularias, astilbes, rodgersias and irises, which would struggle on my lighter soil. Instead I use the low-growing knotweed *Persicaria affinis* 'Dimity' along one edge. This has pink flower spikes which age to red, giving the impression of months of flower. *Origanum vulgare* mingles in the gaps, attracting bees. The neat, double blue *Geranium himalayense* 'Plenum' also does well.

FROGS, TOADS AND NEWTS

Pond vegetation is particularly important to newts, who lay their eggs on water plants in May (here) and protect their eggs by wrapping each one in a leaf, making them impossible to see. I rather discounted the newt as an important creature until ten years ago when I cleared an overcrowded fibreglass pond at the bottom of the garden. I waited until the water level had fallen and began

These newts were discovered hiding under crocosmia leaves in late spring.

bucketing out the water. As the level got lower I struck newts and by the time I'd finished I'd counted well over two hundred common garden newts. The numbers shook me – and I moved them to the pond closer to the house – but it helped to explain why I rarely have a slug problem

Newts are shy creatures. The best way to see them is to take a torch outside during a spring or summer evening and shine it into pond water, searching out the vegetation. From midsummer onwards they spend much of their time out of water, sheltering in cool damp places. During the winter they hibernate in the soil, in the compost heap, under plants and in crevices in stone walls.

Toads and frogs vary in their mating habits. Frogs often spawn in February and lay a ball of eggs. Toads will often wait until late April, and they produce two parallel strands of straight lines and wind it round the vegetation. Toads are squatter and noisier (to my mind) and their Latin name *Bufo bufo* reflects their deep croak. Frogs are smoother, sleeker and more agile.

Toads migrate back to their pond of birth to lay their spawn, many getting killed on the roads as they go. Frogs seem more opportunistic – any pond will do. I have had frogs on my pond, but the frogs seem to come and go, whereas the toad population is consistent and gradually growing

Frogs, toads and newts all feed on invertebrates (including insects), but toads eat a greater percentage of flies than frogs. All three will alleviate your slug problem.

CHAPTER SIX

Bridging the Gap

MAKE SURE THAT YOUR GARDEN CONTINUES TO PROVIDE A SUPPLY
OF NECTAR-RICH FLOWERS, ESPECIALLY DURING THE GAP BETWEEN
SPRING-FLOWERING BULBS AND THE MAIN FLUSH OF PERENNIALS

I f you are to provide food for bees and other insects in your garden, you
will need to know which plants provide nectar. But identifying the
plants that produce lots of nectar isn't as straightforward as it may seem.
Is it a highly scented rose, tightly packed with petals, or the foxglove,
the bluebell or the bright orange Candelabra primula? The answer reveals
some surprising insect choices. The petal-packed rose may have had years of
plant breeding and be highly scented, but all those petals stop pollinators from
accessing the business end of the flower – the stamens and the nectaries
(which contain nectar). As a rule, simply shaped flowers – tubes (as in the
foxglove), bells (as in the bluebell) and saucers (as in the buttercup, mallow or
hardy geranium) – are more attractive to insects than petal-packed flowers.

It's not just the layers of petals that make a double flower a no-go area for
insects. When a plant breeder wants to breed a double, he has to begin with a
plant that shows some disposition to being double, having produced (through
genetic differences) more petals than the usual. In most cases, these extra
petals will have replaced, or partly replaced, the nectaries and the anthers. If
the flower has no nectar source, insects won't visit it.

While simple shapes are more attractive, other flowers lure insects in a
different way. Their flowerheads are made up from hundreds of small individual
flowers. Each of these flowers has a nectary at the base. Some of these tiny
flowers, when massed together, can appear very insect-unfriendly. The teasel
(*Dipsacus fullonum*) and the globe thistle (*Echinops ritro*), for instance, look
almost daunting close up. Touch one and you'll find that they're really prickly
(*echinos* is Greek for hedgehog). Yet bees adore these hard-headed flowers.

The *Umbelliferae* (now *Apiaceae*) or cow parsley family is another group of
plants that produce clusters of tiny flowers. Each flower is supported by its
own stalk and they are often arranged in a domed head. The cow parsleys,

Aquilegia vulgaris var. *stellata* 'Nora Barlow' comes true from seed.

which include angelicas, dill and fennel, are typical umbels: often the showier outer flowers are larger but sterile, and lead the insect to the fertile flowers in the centre. The daisy too – in all its garden forms – has a tight head of flowers in its disc, packed with nectar. The ray florets are purely for show. Thistles, scabious, achilleas, sedums, verbenas and many other garden flowers bear large numbers of tiny flowers packed on to one flowerhead – massed ranks that also indicate a good nectar supply.

As a natural gardener who understands the importance of supplying nectar to sustain bees and insects, you should use these kinds of plants throughout the year, making sure that there are no gaps. There's a period in late spring, sandwiched between the bright crop of spring bulbs and the soft, summer perennials, when the garden tends to be packed with new leaves but to have few flowers. Yet if we go into the countryside, the cow parsley is bursting into life along country lanes and the May tree is showing a hopeful glint of cream in the bud. The insect world, along those lanes, is in rush-

hour mode. Countless solitary bees and hoverflies are after a fix of life-sustaining nectar. You must meet their needs in your garden too then, by having plenty of flowering plants.

Between spring fling and summer bounty

Several hardy geraniums, with saucer-shaped flowers, flower in this late-spring period and make ideal plants for the edge of a woodland garden or other semi-shaded positions. *G. phaeum* is an upright geranium (reaching 36 inches/90 cm) which makes substantial clumps. The dainty, slightly reflexed flowers, carried on long trembling stems to beguiling effect, are most attractive when pure white or deepest purple. When left to self-seed, they come in varying shades of purple and lilac – some like squid ink. Mixed together, though, they give a soft spangled effect to the border.

G. phaeum has a couple of bad habits (most plants do!). It is able to seed and grow within other plants. The seedlings quickly form tight

balls of foliage that fix themselves in the centre of, say, a choice hellebore and prove difficult, or impossible, to winkle out. This makes them unsuitable for small gardens. Their other shortcoming is that they form an untidy mess of stems in winter which doesn't disappear until March. For all that, there are some excellent named sorts available – the lilac 'Lily Lovell' and the pink 'Rose Madder' are well worth finding. *G. phaeum* sets seed abundantly and, usually in June, the finches (green, gold or bull) descend on them with relish. A good cultivar named 'Samobor' has darkly zoned green leaves – marked in deep brown.

G. macrorrhizum is another gap geranium – one with a very different habit. It forms low, lax stems which creep over the ground, covering 24–36 inches (60–90 cm) and rooting as they go. The foliage is always described as aromatic. (It's about as aromatic as a tomcat's urine on a hot day to my mind.) The flower stems, which reach 24 inches (60 cm) at most, come in several colours. The apple blossom ('Ingwersen's Variety'), the magenta ('Bevan's Variety') and white ('Album') are all fine garden plants; and the paler colours are good with late, dark tulips. The foliage is almost evergreen and it colours up well, reddening in late summer. This plant will grow in dense shade, though it is happiest in semi-shade. Also good in shade, and for late spring flowers, are *G. maculatum*, *G. × monacense* (a refined hybrid with *G. phaeum* parentage) and *G. sylvaticum*.

Two other good garden geraniums follow on shortly afterwards. *G. clarkei* 'Kashmir White' has large white saucers finely veined with purple and deeply divided green leaves. This grows well in sun or partial shade and is the best and the earliest of the 'Kashmir' geraniums, all of which reach 24 inches (60 cm). *G. renardii* needs a sunny place. This low-growing geranium (reaching 9 inches/23 cm) has

Above from left A dark form of *Geranium phaeum*; a bullfinch feeding on the seeds of *G. phaeum*; *Chaerophyllum hirsutum* 'Roseum'; *Astrantia* 'Roma'

scalloped sage-green leaves (which last through most of winter) and smallish white flowers veined in purple. Both of these set seed freely. *G. tuberosum*, a sun-lover, also flowers now.

As we have seen, the umbellifers include some of the best nectar plants, particularly for hoverflies and flies. The pink cow parsley *Chaerophyllum hirsutum* 'Roseum' is one of the easiest umbellifers for the late-spring garden, enjoying sunny positions. Most umbellifers are prone to flowering and then dying but this one is a long-lived perennial. Its hard blue pink needs soft blue close by. The later-flowering *Pimpinella major* 'Rosea' needs good moist, fertile soil to thrive – something I'm short of.

Angelica (*A. archangelica*) and sweet cicely (*Myrrhis odorata*) are two more that shine here in early May. They can be tucked into dank spaces and still thrive. The tall biennial angelica reaches 8 feet (2.5 metres) or more and takes its name from a habit of flowering by Archangel Day (8 May). It keeps a presence for months as the large lime-green seeds fade to brown.

My undoubted favourite is a biennial that appears where it will – and some years not at all – in shady, dry areas. *Smyrnium perfoliatum* has the same acid-yellow impact as the euphorbias. The upper perfoliate leaves and umbel are a brash lime yellow that lights up dark corners. The large black seeds should ensure continuity – though (as with many biennials) you will get missed years.

Later in the year the perennial angelicas, such as *A. hispanica*, will flower. I flirt with growing the deep maroon *A. gigas* – surely the handsomest angelica with those striking red

Top *Angelica hispanica*
Bottom *Smyrnium perfoliatum*

heads. This slug-prone plant suffers damage in damp summers and refuses to flower in dry weather. The annual *Orlaya grandiflora* and the perennial selinums provide late-summer flowers.

Gardeners may not realize that astrantias and eryngiums also belong to the umbellifer tribe. Many astrantias flower in May and then repeat flower until autumn. Modern plant breeders have given us *A. major* 'Lars', 'Roma' and the well-known and highly valued 'Hadspen Blood', and *A.m.* subsp. *involucrata* 'Canneman' – useful, very pretty plants that can be tucked away in semi-shade as they enjoy cool moist conditions at the root. One should not forget the hellebore-leaved astrantia (*A. maxima*), a plant that produces pink flowers surrounded by a crisp ruff of bracts. It spreads by rhizomes and is good in moist soil and shade. Astrantias mix well with aquilegias and the hardy blue *Salvia pratensis* Haematodes Group.

The earliest sea holly is the biennial *Eryngium giganteum*. This is a stiff steely plant with a jagged ruff of silver bracts surrounding a tall thimble that allows several bees to feed at once – and they often rest overnight in the cupped bracts. This thimble, made from hundreds of tiny flowers, is an insect magnet for the bumblebee and an essential early-summer plant with presence. Its architectural shape makes it a fine gravel garden plant and it's far earlier than most eryngiums. Like the teasel, it has a hard, spiky head, but though it looks uninviting to us, to a bumblebee it's heaven.

The ultimate test of whether a plant is rich in nectar, if you're in doubt, is to watch the

Euphorbia amygdaloides var. *robbiae* and cultivated bluebells contrast well with the silver-leaved *Elaeagnus* 'Quicksilver'.

bees. Stand by a foxglove for a few seconds and a bee is sure to emerge from an open flower. Each flower has spots or streaks at the throat that are only visible in ultra-violet, and to bees, who pick up ultra-violet light, these nectar guides are like the landing lights at Heathrow. They're as seductive as white high-heeled shoes on brown legs. Plants with spots and streaks on the petals, sometimes visible to us and sometimes not, are an open invitation to bees – come and get me.

Two non-climbing perennial peas are good additions to the garden now, but both need a sunny site. *Lathyrus vernus*, a small, compact plant, can have dark violet flowers and there are all-pink as well as pink and white forms. A more substantial everlasting pea is the golden-orange *L. aureus*. This forms a large clump – at least 24 inches (60 cm) in width – producing many stems packed with flowers. The flowers of both perennial peas (once pollinated) produce long pods of seed – useful for raising new plants.

That cottage garden favourite the aquilegia can really lift the garden in early May and the self-seeders that pop up unannounced are as welcome as carefully positioned plants. I grow several stable strains – coming true from seed – in the garden. I always try to create drifts of these on the woodland edges. The quilled green, white and pink *Aquilegia vulgaris* var. *stellata* 'Nora Barlow' is named after Darwin's granddaughter, who bred aquilegias in her Cambridge garden. The nurseryman Alan Bloom launched the plant and gave it her name in the 1960s, though it is a much older plant and was grown in the sixteenth century. This, though

'China Pink' tulips and honesty

fully double, produces consistent offspring. Sow seeds fresh in late summer and leave to overwinter in a frame.

Equally charming is a large white aquilegia with green tips once known as 'Munstead White' after Gertrude Jekyll's garden but now called *A. vulgaris* 'Nivea'. It lights up the darker areas of the garden, looking very fresh and full of innocence. The ruched purple-black and white *A.v.* 'William Guiness' is another aquilegia which, when planted in a group, adds sparkle to the woodland edges.

There are many named cultivars of *A. vulgaris* – *A.v.* var. *stellata* 'Ruby Port' and 'Greenapples', for instance. Grow several and pollination by the bees will produce serendipitous hybrids. There are also variegated forms and these are easy to grow from seed, though only about half of the seedlings are variegated. They show their variegation on the first true leaves and it's a painless task to select those you want and discard the others. The combination of pink

flower and yellow leaf is the most unwelcome addition to any garden.

Aquilegias are good garden plants for the natural gardener. They grow in shady corners, have good leaves during winter – though you must remove every stem in September to avoid a pile of straw look. Their ability to pop up is a great advantage. Last year several purple aquilegias obligingly posed in front of my golden hop (*Humulus lupulus* 'Aureus') to great effect.

Several other cottage garden favourites contribute now. Some have to be restricted to the wilder edges. Red campion (*Silene dioica*) is one of the jauntiest flowers, but, as with the aquilegias, you will need to restrict the seedlings by removing most or some of the spent flowers – depending on your feelings. Honesty (*Lunaria annua*), a biennial despite its name, not only feeds the bees with nectar by providing lots of flowers: the foliage is also an important food plant for the orange tip butterfly. Honesty grows in dry shade too. Its

Above from left *Aquilegia vulgaris* var. *stellata* 'Ruby Port'; *A. v.* 'Nivea'; *Iris sibirica* 'Silver Edge'

Ranunculus repens var. *pleniflorus*

sun-loving relative sweet rocket (*Hesperis matronalis*) attracts moths with its silver-lavender flowers.

Red valerian (*Centranthus ruber*) will also provide flowers now and colonize rocky walls and dry banks. Buttercups (the refined forms) are worth tucking into damp patches – preferably in sun. The double sort of the running buttercup, *Ranunculus repens* var. *pleniflorus*, strolls through my *Euphorbia griffithii* 'Dixter' in a dull corner of the garden, like frilled buttons. I love the single non-running cream *Ranunculus bulbosus* 'F.M. Burton' and the green-centred, highly frilled double with the very long name *R. constantinopolitanus* 'Plenus' (it looks prettier than it sounds). Similarly dampish areas in semi-shade would be ideal for another May-flowering perennial, *Viola cornuta* Alba Group. This very green-leaved viola has winged white flowers and is long-lived (a rarity with violas). It will send up lots of clean white flowers during May and June and then – after a severe haircut – have a restrained September encore. There are also blue selections of *V. cornuta*.

Some euphorbias form overwintering rosettes of green leaves and many of these flower in early May, enjoying semi-shaded positions. The green-leaved *Euphorbia amygdaloides* var. *robbiae* is a runner – but a controllable one. It produces sulphur-yellow bracts, giving the impression of everlasting flowers, and can light up a dark corner. The wood spurge (*E. amygdaloides*) can look ragged in the garden, but 'Craigieburn' is a more robust form and the combination of lime-green bracts and beetroot-red leaves is a winner in spring. Other euphorbias send up glassy shoots in early spring. Amongst these are the flame-flowered *E. griffithii* and lime-green *E. polychroma* – both good in spring gardens.

The older Siberian irises with willowy leaves and heads of several small flowers – usually in blue – are also early to flower and tolerate shade well. *Iris sibirica* 'Flight of Butterflies', 'Shaker's Prayer', 'White Swirl' and 'Soft Blue' really do tremble like butterflies on the breeze. Plant breeders have produced a new tetraploid race of sturdy, shorter Siberian irises with fatter leaves and larger flowers. Many of these, though lovely, need warmth and sun to flower well. 'Butter and Sugar', 'Silver Edge' and 'Shirley Pope' are all excellent.

The later tulips are great gap flowers. These do not need planting until late October, and can be planted right up until December and still perform. I use tulips in two main areas of my garden. Close to the witch hazels I plant two lily-flowered tulips – 'White Triumphator' and the yellow 'West Point' – against a silver-leaved *Elaeagnus* 'Quicksilver'. There are some bluebells in this area and the combination of the three colours – yellow, blue and white –

'Golden Apeldoorn' tulips and bluebells. Their foliage will soon be covered by the emerging croziers of several ferns.

works well with the silver leaves of this fragrant elaeagnus. Tulips make good companions for autumn-flowering plants. These perennials emerge late and the tulips fill the gaps and give spring colour. I'm still creating my swathe of warm red *Tulipa sprengeri* – always the last to flower – by sprinkling seed on the gravel garden.

The gravel garden is home to several Bearded irises (lovers of sun and warmth). The Bearded irises have been subdivided into six different categories according to their heights – from miniature through to tall. Obligingly the shortest flower first and the tallest last. The shorter varieties make good gravel garden plants, though you must pick strong colours as the pale colours merge into the gravel. 'Sapphire Gem' (an all-blue iris), 'Langport Wren' (a dark magenta purple) and 'Little Blackfoot' (almost black) are three floriferous irises, often flowering in April. These shorter irises do not need constant redivision and keep flowering for a good five years if left to their own devices.

The Hoverfly and Lacewing

Sometimes when spring turns to summer and I have flung open the windows, a lacewing finds itself stranded in the house. This may be the only time I catch sight of one of these delicate creatures with green-veined wings, but visible or not lacewings have an important part to play in the garden. Each adult lives for between 20 and 40 days, feeding on a diet of pollen and honeydew (the sticky substance deposited by aphids). The females lay batches of eggs – from 10 to 30 – and once they hatch the larvae feed on aphids.

The hoverfly, an insect with a steady, hovering flight, follows the same pattern. The adults feed on nectar and pollen, which gives them the necessary energy and protein boost to lay eggs. When the eggs hatch, the larvae feed on the aphids, sucking them dry. Often gardeners confuse hoverflies for bees. This is a deliberate disguise, putting off predators and in the case of some species allowing the hoverfly to scavenge close to the nests and hives of bees.

Anthriscus sylvestris 'Ravenswing', a purple-leaved form of cow parsley

Hoverfly and lacewing flowers

Spring and early summer:

Valerian (*Centranthus ruber*)

Plants of the cow parsley family –
    angelica, smrynium, anthriscus,
sweet cicely (*Myrrhis odorata*)

Single dahlias

Wallflower (*Erysimum*)

Calendula

Nemophila

Doronicum

Sweet William (*Dianthus barbatus*)

Midsummer to autumn:

Yarrow (*Achillea*)

Mint (*Mentha*)

Lavender (*Lavandula*)

Bupleurum fruticosum

Coreopsis

Potentilla

Erigeron

Papaver (produces no nectar
    but is pollen-rich)

Solidago

All daisies, including asters

Centaurea

A shrubby umbellifer, *Bupleurum fruticosum* is a magnet for all flying insects except bees.

SUMMER

CHAPTER SEVEN

The Productive Patch

USE NATURAL RATHER THAN CHEMICAL SOLUTIONS TO PEST PROBLEMS

There's a moment in early summer when the garden hasn't yet peaked, but everything around is burgeoning and full of fresh new life. Young foliage is everywhere – and it's a ready-made gourmet feast for pests of every description. Try not to let the sight of greenfly on your rose buds make you panic and veer towards the chemical section of your garden centre. Resist! Your army of helpers is on hand. Or use a physical solution instead. Wash the blighters away with water, rub them away with your fingers (using gloves if you're squeamish about such things) or leave them for the blue tits to gobble up. Remember that there are many different aphid species and many have specific food plants. They are not going to rampage through your garden like a plague of locusts – trust me.

Carefully watch your plants for signs of infestation and disease and nip any problems in the bud. Remove any diseased leaf and destroy it. Never add it to the compost heap, or you'll perpetuate the disease. Try to keep the air moving around your plants by keeping as many leaves off the ground as possible and by thinning any overcrowded shoots, as moving air currents prevent diseases.

If there is a persistent problem, try to remove it at source by growing something else or by growing your desired plant in a different way. For instance, if slugs slaughter your hostas in the ground, grow them in containers and use a copper band close to the top edge or surround them with grit to keep the beasts away. If your highly bred rose gets black spot every year and you've meticulously tidied every leaf from the ground for at least a couple of years and tar-washed it during winter, replace it with a more robust, disease-free rose such as a Rugosa, Gallica, Alba or Rambler.

If your winter-flowering brassicas always get whitefly, pick off any leaves with the scale-like eggs on the back. If the problem persists, break the cycle by abstaining from growing any brassicas for six months. And remember, if you have got whitefly, those annoying little white specks will sustain many a

Previous page Double opium poppies, soft blue phacelia and *Malva moschata* edge the vegetable patch.
Left Potatoes, shallots, broad beans and peas are surrounded by fruit bushes and flowers.

predatory spider and beetle during the winter months and, come next spring, these predators will be there when you most need them.

The buzz of fresh flavour

You simply can't find the words to describe the taste of just-picked potatoes, runner beans, lettuces, mangetout peas, courgettes and spinach, and you certainly can't buy it on the supermarket shelf. That buzz of fresh flavour makes it well worth finding room for some of the easier-to-grow vegetables in your plot. Even if you can only manage one or two, they'll make life more enjoyable. And if you have a pesticide-free garden you will have no concerns about eating your own produce or feeding it to your family.

Besides the pleasure it provides for the palate, a productive patch can make a handsome feature. Many vegetables, such as cabbages and leeks, are substantial foliage plants in their own right and if you have several of these they will provide a mixture of colours, textures and shapes that is pleasing to the eye. To add even more interest, you can plant the outer edges of a plot with a mixture of flowers, herbs and fruit. The flowers lure plenty of insects into this part of the garden from spring until the first frosts. I also grow rhubarb, autumn-flowering raspberries, gooseberries, redcurrants, strawberries and blackcurrants in my productive plot.

Choosing what to grow

My own small, irregularly shaped productive garden supports the things I like to eat, including new potatoes, mangetout peas, salad leaves, French beans, courgettes, beetroot, early carrots, spinach, runner beans, parsnips and leeks – the sort of vegetables that are best picked and eaten straight away. You will need to make your own choices about what to grow according to your preferences and space.

When choosing from seed catalogues, search for varieties that mention flavour and ignore those described as being for the 'show bench'. Show varieties are bred mostly for uniformity, size and appearance and won't be as good to eat. Then search for varieties with the AGM (Award of Garden Merit) symbol as varieties that have been given this Royal Horticultural Society award have performed well in trials and have been assessed for vigour, flavour and yield.

Catching the moment

Having bought your seeds, when you sow them – according to their individual requirements – the most important part is catching that specific moment when the soil is warm and just moist, for that's when the growth spurt is at its maximum. Conditions vary with each season. Sow too early and your seeds will sit there and sulk. Sow too late and they will miss the boat.

Before sowing, always prepare the soil well, by digging the plot whenever the autumn and winter weather allows you to (but not when the soil's waterlogged). Rake the surface to a fine tilth and allow the soil to settle before sowing.

As my soil is light I incorporate well-rotted cow manure during early spring for three years and then miss a year. This provides me with a rich, airy growing medium. Always avoid treading on your soil in shoes or boots – it compacts the structure – and use a plank to support your weight when planting and digging.

My vegetable schedule runs as follows:

February (if the weather allows)

Sow garlic (bulbs), broad beans and parsnips straight into the ground.

March – the third week

Sow first early potatoes and onion and shallot sets straight into the ground.
Sow salad leaves straight into the ground.
Sow leek and tomato seeds in the greenhouse.

April

Sow mangetout peas, carrots and spinach straight into the ground.

April – late

Sow kale, broccoli, Brussels sprouts, courgettes and squash in the greenhouse.

May – first half

Sow second early peas, spinach and beetroot straight into the ground.

May – second half

Sow climbing French beans and runner beans straight into the ground.

June

Repeat sow any crops I want more of.

July

Sow spring cabbage straight into the ground.

Some helpful tips

Sow all root crops thinly, as the less thinning you have to do the better. Thin in damp conditions when the seedlings are small.

Parsnips take 30 days to germinate. After sowing them in February (or March) oversow the drill with thinly scattered radishes to mark the seeds' position. Be prepared to resow after 30 days. Always use freshly bought parsnip seeds.

When sowing peas, sow them in a zigzag through the trench, using lots of seeds, bearing in mind the old rhyme: 'One for the mouse, one for the crow, one to rot and one to grow.'

Sow runner beans directly into the ground during mid-May, not earlier, using four seeds for each cane. Use an early variety (such as 'Red Rum') and a later one to extend the growing season. Slug damage to runner beans can be devastating – they nip out the growing tip. Use bran, grit and beer traps to discourage them and always sow your beans away from any plants that could shelter slugs – rhubarb, for instance. If slugs are a great problem consider sowing the beans in pots and transplanting them when they reach 9 inches (23 cm) or so in height.

Rotating

Crop rotation is the practice of dividing your vegetables into categories – brassicas (leafy cabbage crops), legumes (peas and beans) and root crops, for example – and growing them in different areas of your plot every year. Rotation prevents many pests and diseases, for two reasons. It avoids the build-up of soil-based pests – carrot root fly, for instance, would always be present in a spot if carrots were grown there year in year out. It also helps the vigour of your crops, as each crop has different nutritional needs. If you grew potatoes in the same place every year they wouldn't yield well, because the previous year's crop would have taken the required nutrients from the soil already. And colonies of pests attracted by potato tubers (such as eelworm and slugs) would be in just the right place to attack the new crop.

Owners of large rectangular plots can rotate their crops easily – using a three- or four-year cycle drawn up on paper. My triangular plot limits me, but I always plant my potatoes where my runner beans grew the year before, fitting in the other rows where possible. This is the nearest I can get to rotation in such a small plot. I fill the gaps with salad crops, shallots and courgettes.

Companion planting

In order to protect my crops I've developed a system of surrounding them with a mixture of nectar-rich flowers and aromatic herbs. Companion planting, as this system is known, is planting so as to benefit from the interaction between different plants when they're grown close together. Though the art has an ancient history – Pliny the Elder recorded his experiences with vines during the first century AD – I had always taken a sceptical view about it, until I had a significant experience with a row of sweet peas. I noticed that several sweet peas growing close to a large fennel plant simply weren't flourishing: they sat still for weeks while every other sweet pea in the row raced away and flowered. This was my first experience of plants interacting. In this case, the highly aromatic fennel was inhibiting the sweet pea. In the same year, a row of carrot seedlings came up with one or two self-seeded aquilegias. The carrots next to the aquilegia seedlings failed to develop. Since that fateful year, I've restricted flowering plants (including herbs) to the outer edges of my vegetable patch, just in case they inhibit the growth of certain vegetables.

Later that summer, my brassica plants were totally ignored by the cabbage white butterflies – although plenty of them seemed to be flying overhead. Normally I have to cover all my brassicas with fine mesh to avoid their demise, but that year they remained untouched. My cabbage plants were growing next to a row of sage plants (*Salvia officinalis*). I have concluded that pungent plants (including those of the onion family) mask the smell of carrots, brassicas and beans – and so keep away predators. Here are some examples of pungent plants that act as insect repellents:

- Lavender under apple trees prevents the codling moth.
- Nasturtiums under apple trees discourage woolly aphid.
- Chives close to carrots keeps root fly away.
- Garlic and nasturtiums repel aphids.
- Onions repel carrot and cabbage flies (but inhibit peas).
- Mint repels cabbage white butterflies and flea beetles (strew it about rather than plant it) on brassicas.
- Tomatoes, sage, rosemary, hyssop, thyme, mint, tagetes, chives, alliums, artemisia and lavender keep the caterpillars away from brassicas.
- Summer savory protects broad beans from blackfly.

I have also observed that some plants thrive when planted together. Here are some examples:

- Carrots and peas do well together.
- Onions enjoy growing with beetroot, lettuce, cabbages, carrots, apple trees and rose bushes.
- Raspberries and rue do well together.
- Tomatoes crop heavily when planted with pot marigolds.
- Beans do well with carrots, beets and cauliflower.
- Broad beans and early potatoes always do well together.

Nectar-rich flowers for the productive plot

The flowers at the outer edges of my plot include edible plants – pot marigolds, borage and nasturtiums – for salads, garnish and for drinks. I remove any poisonous or toxic plants – all members of the buttercup family and foxgloves, for instance – in case they find their way into salads. I also grow nectar-rich flowers designed to attract pollinating and predatory insects – particularly hoverflies, because they (together with the bees) pollinate the fruit and vegetable crops and their larvae eat aphids.

Scatter-and-sow annuals

Mix up packets of seed (or self-saved seed) of some or all of the following plants into a container and wait for a damp, warm day in late March or early April. Lightly fork through the soil to encourage any seeds lurking in the soil to germinate. Sprinkle the seeds over the soil in waves, not straight lines. Water with warm water (in the morning if possible) on dry days. Within three weeks you should have lots of seedlings.

Poached egg plant (*Limnanthes douglasii*) is useful as a low-growing, scatter-and-sow border edge. It flowers in early May, before the main flush of annuals. It will disappear by midsummer, then reseed itself.

Orlaya grandiflora – a lacy umbel that produces white flowers from June onwards. Save the large brown seeds at the end of the summer and resow by scattering on the ground during spring. Pot marigold (*Calendula officinalis*) – bright orange and yellow daisies in varying warm colours, styles and heights, from neat doubles to ragged quills. Deadhead to keep it in flower and leave some plants to self-seed – but also collect some seeds to scatter in spring.

Phacelia tanacetifolia – a soft mauve, arching flowerhead set above finely cut foliage. This will self-seed and can be dug in as a green manure crop at the end of winter. Highly popular with bumblebees.

Opium poppy (*Papaver somniferum*) – a glaucous-leaved plant that produces large, often double flowers in June. Remove most of the seedheads during summer, allowing a few

From left *Papaver somniferum; Phacelia tanacetifolia; Scabiosa columbaria*

to self-seed. Sprinkle saved seed in the spring. Poppies provide a source of protein-rich pollen essential for egg production.`

Love-in-a-mist (*Nigella damascena*) – treat in the same way as the opium poppy as this can also set far too many seeds.

Plants to sow in trays and then transplant or to buy as bulbs

Some of the following need to be sown under glass. A cold frame in a warm sheltered place is just as effective as a greenhouse.

Ornamental alliums – the tall *A. hollandicum* 'Purple Sensation' produces round mauve flowerheads in May, setting the ball rolling. Remove the seedhead before it drops the seed – usually in August. 'Purple Sensation' is a really lovely addition to the vegetable patch. The September-flowering garlic chive (*A. tuberosum*) has bright green leaves and white flowers and is popular with all insects.

Dianthus barbatus 'Sooty' – a dark-flowered form of the sweet William, a biennial. Sow outdoors during June and July and transplant the young plants outside during September and they will flower during their second summer. 'Noverna Purple' (the name comes from 'no vernalization', meaning that the seed does not require a period of cooling before germination is possible) is a unique annual form of sweet William with bright pink-purple heads. This can be sown early in the year and will flower during the same year.

Single dahlias can be seed-raised under glass in early spring or you can buy named varieties (such as the 'Bishop of Llandaff') as tubers. Plant out in May. The single forms are very attractive to hoverflies, the doubles less so. All flower from June until the first frosts.

Gloriosa daisies (*Rudbeckia hirta*) are late-summer flowering annuals in shades of yellow, orange and brown. Sow under glass in March and plant out when large enough. They flower late into the year and sometimes survive the winter and flower again the following year.

Agastache foeniculum – an aromatic member of the mint family which produces a spike of blue flowers, but rarely overwinters. Sow under glass for late-summer flowers.

Sweet peas (*Lathyrus odoratus*) can be sown in deep pots (8 inches/20 cm or more) during early

March, under glass, and planted outside in April, supported by canes, either in rows or climbing tripods. They should flower by early July.

Half-hardy annuals

Nasturtiums can be sown directly into the ground in early May, to flower from midsummer onwards. Don't sow them any earlier as they are very susceptible to frost damage.

Perennials

Deadheading will keep these going for weeks.

Scabiosa columbaria – a native plant, producing masses of small flowers (from midsummer onwards) which are highly popular with bumblebees.

Linaria triornithophora produces slender wands of deep violet-blue flowers (July onwards) and takes its name from the arrangement of flowers, *tri ornis* meaning three birds.

Musk mallow (*Malva moschata*) – a short-lived perennial that produces saucers of white or pink flowers from June onwards and self-seeds.

Knautia macedonica – a scabious with maroon-red flowers (June onwards).

Decoy plants

Along the plot edge I use two decoy plants which lure predators away from the vegetables. French marigolds (*Tagetes patula*) close to my salad leaves attract every slug for miles. Nasturtiums attract cabbage white butterflies – giving an early warning about their presence – and help to protect your brassicas from aphids for a short time.

Herbs

Around the edges of the vegetable plot I fit sage, rosemary, lavender, rocket and parsley. I allow mint to grow under the autumn-flowering raspberries, which are separated from the main area by a path. Mint is invasive, but I have never suffered from raspberry flea beetle and the raspberries are strong enough to survive – so far. Ladybirds shelter in the large sage plants during winter, so the sage ensures that they stay in this part of the garden, ready to attack any pests in early spring.

Above from left Pot marigold; tagetes; nasturtium; a cabbage white caterpillar munching a nasturtium leaf

SLUGS

Slugs thrive in our cool temperate climate and they can cause devastation, reducing a row of young lettuce or newly planted bedding to a row of stalks, and testing every gardener – even organic ones – to the limit of their patience. Most slugs, like dirty old men, go for the young and fresh and are most frisky in spring. And there is no magic solution. The use of slug pellets is not the answer. They will not only poison every slug and snail in your garden but also, more importantly, find their way into the bodies of songbirds, amphibians, beetles and hedgehogs. Eating a lot of pellets can kill household pets. Dogs can be indiscriminate feeders and as pellets contain the same cereal base as dog food they find them attractive. The chemical soon gets washed out of the pellet by rainwater. So please do not use them.

It's vital to remember two things. Firstly, slugs are active from dusk through the night, rarely emerging during the day. This means that watering in the evening – when most gardeners resort to the can, hose and sprinkler – helps them to glide across the soil to a damp dinner. It's therefore best to avoid watering plants in the late evening.

Secondly, there are thirty species of slug in the UK and I want you to remember that old spaghetti western *The Good, the Bad and the Ugly* when you think about slugs because the title describes them perfectly. The large black slugs, which are very, very large and confusingly come in a range of shades, send a shiver down your back and are definitely ugly. They clear lots of debris – old leaves and spent petals – from the garden and rarely cause severe harm to new plants. They are mostly useful creatures and are much more mobile than most slugs. Preserve them.

The bad are only too familiar, as they munch the growing tips off plants, chew through the main stems and eat our potatoes. The three real baddies are:

European grey field slug (*Deroceras reticulatum*) – usually a fawny-grey, feeds close to the soil surface and eats everything, including roots. There are three generations in most years.

Keeled slug (*Tandonia budapestensis*) – spends most of its time underground, munching potatoes, carrots and any other edible roots. You can identify these dark, almost black, slugs by the thin orange line down their backs.

Garden slug (*Arion hortensis*) – usually black with a pale underside and is all consuming. This is the one that often nips the growing points out of beans.

The good – a slug that doesn't touch vegetation and actually eats other slugs, including the keeled slug and the garden slug – is the testacella slug (*Testacella haliotidea*). It has a little mussel-shaped shell on its back – about the size of a little fingernail. You're not likely to see a testacella slug unless you are double digging or emptying a compost heap, as they rarely come to the surface and live deep in the soil.

How to discourage slugs

- Make sure that you're scrupulous about removing spent vegetative material from the garden – old cabbage stumps, fading rhubarb leaves, yellowing leaves close to vulnerable plants like young vegetables and seedlings.
- When planting newly raised young plants, harden them off for a week outside first, as vegetation straight from the greenhouse is far too tempting.
- Cover new plants with plastic water bottles, each cut off at the bottom with the lid on and buried in the ground to make a mini-cloche.
- Leave wide gaps between rows of vegetables. These will enable you to hoe the soil and disturb slugs' eggs. Disturbing the top 4 inches (10 cm) of the soil is a very effective control.
- Avoid mulching with grass clippings, plastic or mesh – these make a perfect home for slugs.
- Spread grit, bran and eggshells close to vulnerable plants.
- Some gardeners use beer traps – but I don't drink beer.
- Night-time patrols are the most effective way of dealing with slugs. I have a disposal kit of rubber gloves, a torch and a container – my preferred container is a jam jar. In the fading daylight I gather up the slugs in the jar and stamp on them with heavy boots. I repeat this process every evening during spring and summer. Decoy plants planted close to the edge of the vegetable patch make gathering them up easier.
- Apply nematodes to the vegetable patch in warm weather (over 15°C/59°F) when the soil is moist in late spring and early autumn.

Snails tend to do less harm, but they feed during the day. I just gather these up when I see them. In cool, wet summers they can wreak havoc on dahlias. A good tip is to leave a small piece of paving or a flat stone at the back of borders every 30 feet (10 metres) or so. These make perfect anvils for thrushes, who are by far the most efficient predator of snails.

CHAPTER EIGHT

Here Comes Summer

GET TO KNOW YOUR SOIL AND ACCEPT ITS LIMITATIONS,
GROWING MANY DIFFERENT KINDS OF THE PLANTS THAT THRIVE
NATURALLY IN YOUR AREA, CHEEK BY JOWL

I dream about growing masses of old-fashioned roses, but my thin, stony soil dries out far too much and even if I enriched the soil with huge amounts of cow manure and mulched with spent grass clippings on a weekly basis most of the more demanding old-fashioned roses would still fail spectacularly. I compromise and stick to growing Ramblers, Rugosas, Albas, shrub roses and Gallicas – the less demanding roses.

Your garden will restrict you in similar ways. Heavy clay, for example, doesn't suit silvery, aromatic lavender or sun-loving pinks, which need sharp drainage, and though you might be able to create a raised bed full of grit to house a few, most of your garden would be best planted with clay-loving perennials and shrubs. Roses (even those old-fashioned beauties), viburnums, hostas, phlox, monardas and asters will love your garden. Accept your limitations – and by doing so you will avoid plant stress and reduce the incidence of disease caused by water stress – be it waterlogging or drought.

When you have decided what you can grow – remembering that the best research is to look at gardens close to you – grow your plants cheek by jowl, aiming to cover the soil completely by midsummer. A leafy canopy of plants is the best conserver of water, shading the soil from the drying summer sun. Ground beetles will happily scurry through your shady borders, devouring pests as they go. Borders which have each plant surrounded by a ring of bare soil are anathema to the insect world. They don't want to have to cross a mini-desert every time they move. Growing as many different plants as you can will attract more insect life, both in the air and on the ground.

The sweetest moment

The summer solstice (21 June) rewards the gardener with eighteen hours of daylight (in my part of the world) and by now my garden is full of flowering

The most admired part of my garden is the cottage garden border.

Pink valerian, emerging verbascums and angelica in the cottage garden border.

plants, glorying in those long days. My cottage garden border, full of summer-flowering perennials and hardy cottage garden annuals, is the hub of the garden at this, the sweetest moment in the gardening year. As the border starts to decline, I add tender plants – dahlias, nicotianas and salvias – but although this extends the life of the border by a few weeks, the cottage garden border never looks quite as sumptuous as it did in midsummer – but that's gardening, folks!

Soft summer colours and grey-green foliage abound here. There are peachy, Oriental poppies, pale blue catmint, soft green angelicas, pallid yellow daisies and hemerocallis. Touches of white appear, courtesy of the thuggish white willow herb (*Chamerion angustifolium* 'Album') – which I adore; if you feel threatened by spreading roots, though, this is not a plant for you. The border's not all pale and pastel. Lacquered scarlet ladybird poppies and cobalt-blue cornflowers add a bolt of vibrancy wherever they appear. Some are planted deliberately and others have self-seeded.

Many gardeners shun the herbaceous border as being far too labour intensive. Visions of having to divide and replant every second year or so come to mind. This was necessary for the country house gardeners who used to create long narrow borders packed against a hedge with plants such as phlox and asters. Choose your perennials wisely, however, and they'll survive without division. Oriental poppies (*Papaver orientale*), nepetas, hardy geraniums, kniphofias, crocosmias, rudbeckias, echinacea, sanguisorbas, hemerocallis and alliums can remain undisturbed for ten years – and probably longer. It's only Tall Bearded irises, grown towards the front of the border, that need a regular divide and replant every third year.

The largest, blowziest flowers belong to the Oriental poppies (*Papaver orientale*). This diverse group of plants (bred from at least four species) produces flowers in shades of white, pink, peach, plum, lilac, orange and bright red in a variety of habits and heights. I avoid any bright orange Oriental poppies as they are always difficult to place, really only blending with deep blue or warm yellow.

All Oriental poppies behave in the same way. The new leaves appear during autumn and make a welcome foliage feature for the first six months of the year, when so much is dormant. The downside is that the leaves disappear again by late summer and leave a maddening gap. A gap that demands to be filled! I use dahlias, salvias or tobacco plants, planting them round the crown of the poppy. This palaver is worth it, for the crêpe-like petals of the Oriental poppy capture the freshness of summer perfectly and the bird's-eye view of those black blotches surrounding the maroon-velvet seedhead is one of the sights of summer. When their moment of glory is over, I cut them hard back to the

Papaver orientale 'Raspberry Queen'

ground and don't allow them to self-seed, so as to keep the vigour in the plant. All Oriental poppies are strong, long-lived plants and you can increase them by taking root cuttings in late winter.

The earliest poppy to flower here is the dusky, sultry 'Patty's Plum' – an upright, sturdy, tall poppy that likes some shade. It pushes up through the corkscrew stems of a contorted hazel (*Corylus avellana* 'Contorta'), timing its flowers to coincide with the emerging oh-so-green hazel leaves. This poppy has petals of warm plum – muted to the colour of faded velvet – and it's much admired here. 'Lilac Girl' a seedling from 'Patty's Plum', has a similar faded elegance but is much bluer and cooler in colour – but not lilac, despite its name. Another colour-blind male nurseryman! (This is not sexist – far more men are colour-blind than women.)

Equally upright in habit (reaching to almost 36 inches/90 cm) is 'Raspberry Queen', once described by my favourite nurseryman, Bob

Brown of Cotswold Garden Flowers, as 'Barbara Cartland with running mascara, leaning slightly' – a description I've never bettered. The silver-green leaves frame the bright pink poppies perfectly and mature plants keep their upright habit, making a tightly waisted clump (something we should all aspire to in maturity). Also on the tall and upright side is the scarlet-red 'Beauty of Livermere'. I love this 'not a hint of pink to be seen' red in the garden – all warmth and colour.

Marcus Perry, a nurseryman who grew huge numbers of perennial plants at the beginning of the twentieth century, bred the first non-orange Oriental poppies. Two of his creations – the soft salmon-pink 'Mrs Perry' and the all-white 'Perry's White' – are tried and tested garden performers, reaching just 24 inches (60 cm) or so in height. They make wider plants, blending well into other perennials. Two more modern additions to my poppy collection are the lavender-white 'Graue Witwe' or Grey Widow – a ghostly flower that reaches about 24 inches (60 cm). Another, the grey-pink 'Cedric Morris' – a similar height – is a restrained grower. I know that Oriental poppies are all divas, rather than good-value, long-term chorus plants, but they're showstoppers and leave me wanting more.

There are several stiff upright swords in this border to balance the roundly curvaceous poppies. Tall Bearded irises are always difficult to sustain in a mixed border as they need the sun at their feet if they're to flower. I contrive to grow them at the front edges. The tall all-blue iris in my border has grown in this garden for over twenty years – possibly longer – and (as with many irises) the name is long-forgotten. A good modern alternative is 'Jane Phillips' – pale blue with a silvery gleam. The sword-like grey-green leaves of all Bearded irises make a feature long after the flowers have faded.

In order to understand an iris catalogue it's important to know that the falls are the three downward-facing petals, the standards are the three upright petals and the beard is the fluffy growth on the falls. Picotees have a darker edge to the petals and selfs are all one colour. New

American irises are often tetraploids and they have lots of enormous flowers on one stem, up to fourteen, and are too top-heavy for my taste and for my garden. They don't blend into a border and they certainly need staking – something I try to avoid.

I've stuck to blue and purple irises and I also grow 'Katie-Koo' (a violet-purple Intermediate with a grey beard), and 'Braithwaite', a classic Tall Bearded iris with pale blue standards and dark blue velvet falls. The range of colours available gives you plenty of scope and I'm aware that I should be more adventurous in my choices.

I use crocosmias, very easy trouble-free plants, in this border. The July-flowering, bright red 'Lucifer' is mouthwatering. The mid-green pleated leaves perfectly balance the vibrant red. These flowers fade within two or three weeks but many crocosmias perform for longer, though perhaps not as spectacularly.

C. masoniorum (a parent of 'Lucifer') has more branching, taller flower spikes, reminiscent of a seagull in flight. The flowers open over a month or more and the dark chocolate seedheads keep the show going – but the flower colour is altogether subtler and more burnished than that of the fiery 'Lucifer'. Many crocosmias flower later in the season – C. × *crocosmiiflora* 'Star of the East' and 'Dusky Maiden' are both late. As a rule of thumb I find that the oranges are tougher than the yellows as far as hardiness is concerned.

Daylilies also provide strappy leaves and I like the old-fashioned, airy yellow varieties with slender, fragrant trumpets. The fragrant *Hemerocallis lilioasphodelus* (syn. *H. flava*) wins a place in my border because it flowers so early in the year – at the same time as the aquilegias. I also grow the elegant, pale yellow 'Whichford', the shorter remontant golden-yellow 'Stella De Oro', the long-flowering

Above from left *Geranium* Rozanne ('Gerwat'); *G. himalayense* 'Plenum'; *G. pratense* 'Mrs Kendall Clark'; *G.p.* 'Striatum' (often sold commercially as 'Splish-splash')

Crocosmia 'Lucifer', a mouth-watering combination of red flowers and fresh green leaves

'Golden Chimes' (a plant with dark stems and buds) and the pale yellow 'Corky'.

In recent years the hemerocallis has undergone a transformation at the hands of mainly American plant breeders, who work on the basis of the bigger and brasher the better and have produced sturdy tetraploid plants in every shade imaginable. These newer hemerocallis often have large flat flowers and usually bloom in the second half of summer. I'm trying to like them, and I've got some of these power-packed hemerocallis – 'Chicago Sunrise', for instance – but I find them hard to place.

Kniphofias are useful for extending the flowering season as many of the yellow varieties flower from late summer onwards and their strappy foliage is a year-round feature – though it always needs a thorough tidy by spring. 'Percy's Pride' is a floriferous cool lime-yellow poker, 'Tetbury Torch' is a warmer yellow and 'Wrexham Buttercup' is a golden yellow with a green tinge. All three are easy, but can suffer from snail damage during wet summers. Regular frisking for snails should be a weekly task.

Strong rigid verticals, reaching up into the sky, are an essential in any border. These tall spires should not be tucked away at the back: let them rise up at the front of the border as well. The spikes of grey-leaved verbascums are great favourites of mine. They form a felted silver-white spire in early summer and then produce acid-yellow flowers that erupt randomly up the spike for most of the summer. Finally they leave their magnificent silhouette late into the winter as they die.

Last year I grew the multi-branched *V. bombyciferum* 'Silver Lining' – more tree than flower. It can be sown in spring and may well flower that year – or it may wait until next year. Moderate self-seeding usually produces some new plants, but it's best to save and sow some seed in trays. The only long-lived perennial verbascum I have known is *V. chaixii*, but this fresh-faced verbascum lacks the architectural structure of the candelabra-like biennial *V. bombyciferum*.

I also like to grow angelicas for their sturdy frames. The most commonly grown species, *A. archangelica* can reach 8 feet (2.5 metres) in height and that can be overbearing. The shorter, glossy-leaved *A. pachycarpa* (syn. *A. hispanica*) reaches only 24–36 inches (60–90 cm) and is much more useful among other flowers. Angelicas are difficult to define as they form a rosette during their first year and flower in their second – a biennial trait; yet sometimes they can live for three or four years before they succumb. To be safe, always save some seed and sprinkle it into the border. The large corky angelica seeds can be tricky in pots. They are attractive to mice and their corky covering holds water and they can succumb to rot. Lie them on their edge to aid drainage and cover the pots to keep away the mice.

Ornamental alliums come in a variety of shapes and sizes, some too delicate for a border. The sturdy *A. cristophii* is a reliable year-on-year performer, producing starry mauve

Hemerocallis 'Jenny Wren'

flowerheads in early June. Later the drumstick allium (*A. sphaerocephalon*) produces small tight pink-crimson heads that last for several weeks. These are good value as the seedheads endure for months. Alliums have the added advantage that they can be pot grown and then planted in the border to plug the gaps.

Amongst the sturdy stems, spires and swords there are several flowers that tremble and move. The giant lemon scabious *Cephalaria gigantea* reaches over 8 feet (2.5 metres) in height and the branching hollow stems and large divided leaves are topped with lemon-yellow, frilly-edged flowers – their green centres flecked with black. This makes a wonderful cut flower and a moving background

of subtle colour at the back of the border – where it emerges in cold, shaded soil. You need to deadhead this plant thoroughly straight after flowering, as unwanted seedlings quickly make large tap-rooted plants that sometimes infiltrate other treasures.

Perhaps my favourite plant in the whole border is a slender, tall form of great burnet called *Sanguisorba officinalis* 'Arnhem' . This wonderful plant produces tall, wiry stems (reaching 4 feet/1.2 metres or more) of maroon-red bobbles. As summer fades, these round heads dry to brown black, maintaining a permanent presence in the border. One nurseryman has described this plant as 'a swarm of wasps in mid-flight'.

Two other low-growing sanguisorbas with maroon flowers and pinnate foliage are *S.o.* 'Tanna' and *S. menziesii*. The flowers are longer, fluffier and fatter on both and neither have the lasting presence of 'Arnhem'. However, 'Arnhem' (bred by Piet Oudolf) is still hard to find. There is also a tall, white sanguisorba with very divided, green leaves called S.

tenuifolia 'Alba'. The stamen-covered, fluffy white flowers are like waving pennants, reaching 2 inches (5 cm) in length, and make a good white flower – but like almost all white flowers they brown as they fade.

There are many pink sanguisorbas, but some have glaucous foliage which jars against the soft greenery of early summer. *S. obtusa* has very ornate, highly serrated grey-green leaves (sometimes drawing comparison with the magnificent foliage of *Melianthus major*). The hard blue-pink flowers and greyish leaves are perfect with old-fashioned roses, but not so good in my border of mainly soft green leaf.

A Chinese species called *S. hakusanensis* makes a substantial border plant, but is far clumsier and coarser in habit. 'Pink Lipstick', a new introduction, has neat bright pink flowers against good leaves and another, 'Pink Elephant', has waving horizontal flowers arched like an elephant's trunk. If you haven't grown any sanguisorbas, search them out.

I allow several flowers to seed down. These include aquilegias (which seem to be in shades

of maroon and white just here), campion, valerian, linaria and fennel. I restrict the fennel to the part of the border where *Crocosmia* 'Lucifer' grows as they make a good combination together. I allow the valerian – always pink despite my various attempts to introduce the red and white – in another area. Deadheaded, this cottage garden favourite will last all summer.

Linaria purpurea is prevalent in this garden, but there is a good white cultivar ('Springside White' – the only plant I know that started life in Hook Norton) and a pink ('Canon Went'). Any unwanted self-seeding purple linarias can easily be removed. Campions – both white and red – also pop up, but I remove the seed capsule of every plant before it scatters its seed. I also grow two annuals – blue cornflowers (*Centaurea cyanus* 'Blue Diadem') and ladybird poppies (*Papaver commutatum*) – to fill the gaps. I sow the seeds of this poppy under glass – the tiniest pinch in a 3 inch

(7 cm) flower pot – and transplant the plants in late April. This is bending the rules, as poppy seed is best sprinkled on the garden, but I can't bear to risk being without this plant. I prick out the cornflowers into single pots and by deadheading both it's possible to keep them flowering for three months or more. I sprinkle seeds of the silvery, pale Mother of Pearl Group poppies through the border and these come up as and when. Using ephemerals such as these can unify a border and make the planting more natural, so in order to encourage them I never mulch this area of the garden.

Two Gallica roses grow in this border: the striped *R.g.* 'Versicolor' and the deep pink 'Surpasse Tout'. Though they only flower once, in June, they add an old-rose charm. Later in the summer the soft apricot 'Buff Beauty' – the best of the Hybrid Musk roses to my mind – produces lots of flowers in flushes, which continue until late autumn. Close by, two double cultivars of the drought-tolerant

Above from left *Rosa* 'Paul's Himalayan Musk'; *R.* Bonica ('Meidomonac'); *R. gallica* 'Versicolor'; *R.* 'Roseraie de l'Haÿ'

Clematis viticella scramble and creep gently through the roses. 'Purpurea Plena Elegans' is a soft pink-red irregular pom-pom with touches of green and 'Mary Rose' is a dark purple. Their small flowers – about 1½ inches (4 cm) in diameter – may reach the silver leaves of the weeping pear (*Pyrus salicifolia* 'Pendula') or the well-behaved, small *Buddleja* 'Lochinch' – if I'm lucky.

In June, two closely related, upright hardy geraniums flower at the back of the border. *G. psilostemon* has magenta flowers with a dark eye and 'Patricia' (*G. endressii* × *G. psilostemon*) produces almost identical flowers, but for a much longer period. A new geranium called Rozanne ('Gerwat') produces huge, powder-blue flowers (well over an inch across) on a sprawling plant – beginning in June and going on until October. This is a sterile hybrid resulting from two closely related species – something that often happens with geraniums. Rozanne is unable to set seed and as a result flowers on and on at the front of the border.

Hardy geraniums come in shades of white, mauve, blue and magenta and blend into cottage garden borders, needing little attention. Nepetas have the same ability, although almost all are blue. 'Six Hills Giant', a silver-leaved aromatic nepeta, is also sterile, flowering for months on end. It's a fine foil for other plants, including roses.

In late summer the cottage garden border relies on purple coneflowers (echinaceas), rudbeckias and leucanthemums – all daisies that enjoy moisture-retentive soil. Echinaceas can be seed-raised in early spring; they will flower during the same year and you can place these new plants in the border in July if needed. The front-of-the-border spreader *Rudbeckia fulgida* var. *sullivantii* produces lots of bright yellow daisies, each studded with a dark brown eye. The leaves are rich green and the plant shines in August – a rare commodity.

Leucanthemums – a genus of plants who've been well and truly shuffled by the botanists – are better known as Shasta daisies. Most are a stark white – a difficult colour to place. L. × *superbum* 'Sonnenschein' has the holly-green leaves of other leucanthemums, but the daisies are custard-cream yellow and if deadheaded it carries on flowering late into the year.

By late summer, I will have plugged any gaps with drought-resistant flower-packed penstemons in dark colours – 'Blackbird', 'Garnet' and 'Raven' – as they carry on until October and are flattered by the clear September light.

This crescent-shaped border doesn't contain any spring bulbs and I usually leave it intact until February. Then the textures between the spikes, the swords and the airy flowers can be enjoyed once again – when the frost rimes the seedheads. A few teasels grow at the back and they pull in goldfinches anxious to eat their large black seeds.

Clockwise from top left *Clematis viticella* 'Purpurea Plena Elegans'; *C.* 'Mary Rose'; *C.* 'Etoile Violette'; *C.* 'Polish Spirit'

THE HONEYBEE

A honeybee on garlic chives

Originally, honeybees (*Apis mellifera*) came from the warmer parts of Asia, which is why they can only fly in warm temperatures. This makes them less effective pollinators than the bumblebees – who can fly in cool conditions. They are also limited by the length of their tongues, which aren't long enough to pollinate some flowers. They prefer saucer-shaped and dish-shaped flowers of simple construction. They are also unable to buzz pollinate flowers as the bumblebee does to release the pollen.

Although the honeybees can't fly on cool mornings or chilly evenings and aren't nearly as industrious as the bumblebee, they are useful pollinators in other respects. They live in elaborate hives and each colony may have as many as 50,000 bees. They communicate with each other, via their bee dance, and concentrate their efforts on a small area – collecting pollen from one type of plant at a time. They make fewer visits than bumblebees during each individual foray from their hive, but honeybees collecting nectar from apple trees, for instance, will continue to visit the crop until the nectar supply is exhausted. This means that a fruit crop or a vegetable crop is pollinated much more reliably by honeybees than by bumblebees.

Many colonies of honeybees are kept commercially and used for the production of honey and the honeybees in your garden probably come from a managed hive – even if you live in a town or a city. In the wild, colonies of honeybees are sometimes found in hollow trees.

Honeybees love round, saucer-shaped flowers. The hollyhock, the evening primrose and the mallow are all popular. Under ultra-violet light the flowers of the apparently clear yellow evening primrose are highly streaked with a darker colour – and these nectar guides lead the bee to the middle of the flower.

In a trial held at the Cambridge University Botanic Garden during 1997 (funded by English Nature) of the twenty-four plants monitored the following were the most popular with the honeybee (listed in order of popularity):

Musk mallow (*Malva moschata*)
Common mallow (*Malva sylvestris*)
Lesser scabious (*Scabiosa columbaria*)
Cornflower (*Centaurea cyanus*)
Wild clary (*Salvia verbenaca*)

The white form of *Malva moschata*

A Word About the Wasp

The wasp is a meat-eating bee and a useful garden predator – not a pest. There are also lots of tiny, parasitic wasps in our gardens, some of which are used for the biological control of pests.

Some Colour Preferences

The most important pollinators in order of importance are bees, flies, butterflies and moths, and beetles. All insect-pollinated plants tend to be colourful and sometimes fragrant, but insects have different colour vision from ours. Most can detect ultra-violet as a separate colour but few can detect red – with the exception of the butterfly. To most insects, red appears grey.

Insect-pollinated flowers tend to be yellow, orange, white or blue. The pollinators have different preferences, however. Bees are attracted to yellow and white flowers, butterflies to red, pink and purple. Flies like flowers with a meaty odour, which often come in insignificant colours such as green, white and reddish brown. Moths are attracted to white and mauve flowers, many of which are fragrant and secrete their nectar during the evening.

CHAPTER NINE

The Hotter the Better

AVOID WATERING BY ADAPTING YOUR PLANTING TO INCLUDE
PLENTY OF DROUGHT-TOLERANT PLANTS IN DRY PLACES AND USE
A VARIETY OF DIFFERENT MULCHES TO TRAP THE MOISTURE

Visitors to the garden often tell me that I must have good soil and that I must be constantly watering to have a flower-filled garden; yet, as I have said, my garden has dry, stony soil – and I only water containers and some vegetables. Water is a precious resource in the garden, even in apparently rainy Britain, and we shouldn't be encouraged to pour it on the garden unnecessarily. I don't water because I use mulches, which keep moisture in. The sunniest, driest parts of the garden contain sun-lovers planted in gravel, an effective mulch – but different materials can be used in different areas of the garden. Bark blends particularly well with woodlanders – pulmonarias and hellebores – though the blackbirds are sure to pick through it and scatter it about. Spent grass clippings (rotted in the sun for a day or so) can be used under raspberries, with runner beans and at the back of borders, to stop the sun and wind from drying out the soil. The golden rule when mulching is apply only when the soil is damp and warm – never when it's dry. The mulch is there to keep moisture in, not keep the rain out.

As grass and bark rot down, the process uses up nitrogen reserves at soil level. Therefore you must apply a top dressing of a fertilizer (blood, fish and bone, or hoof and horn) to replenish the nitrogen before you add the mulch. Mulches suppress all seed germination and weeds are less likely to grow, but mulch will also stop annual plants and others you may want to self-seed from doing so. You have to think carefully about what you want to achieve.

Gravel has the added advantage that it doesn't rot down, but you may not wish to use it if you have young children who might fall over on this unfriendly surface. It tends to disappear back into the soil, though, and needs replenishing every third year or so. A gravel mulch works in two ways. It seals the moisture into the soil during summer – and in sun-baked areas this is very desirable – and

The silky fronds of *Stipa barbata* flow over the silver leaves in the gravel garden.

Stipa barbata, Dierama pulcherrimum and *Eryngium giganteum* in the gravel garden

acts as a drainage material during winter. When adding new plants to a gravel bed, the technique is to scrape away as much of the gravel from the planting site as possible, making a heap. Then remove the soil due to be displaced by the plant and put it straight into a bucket. Plant your new treasure and rake the gravel around the plant, and place the spare soil in another part of the garden. I do leave spaces between each plant in the bed – to allow myself room to scrape back the gravel. Gravel is a good medium for self-seeding plants – sometimes too good. *Eryngium giganteum, Geranium robustum* and *G. pratense* have to be thinned out at the seedling stage.

When you plant sun-loving plants capable of thriving in very dry conditions it is imperative to water them during their first growing season – using a can is best. This is because their survival is due to an enormously deep root system that may stretch 5 feet (1.5 metres) or more below the ground. Obviously, this root system takes time to establish and until it's in place you must sustain the plant.

High summer

In high summer in the gravel garden tall grasses and dieramas sway over a sea of silvery leaves – lavenders, achilleas and artemisias. Though it's full of flowers, it never needs any water – in fact the hotter the better. There's nothing magical about this. Hot dry conditions suit a whole range of plants, most of them with specially adapted leaves or roots. Plants with finely divided leaves (artemisias, pinks and carnations) and those with aromatically oily leaves (lavender, sage and rosemary) are two types that thrive in full sun. Some plants have hairy leaves (verbascums and salvias) and others have fleshy plump leaves (the sedum and the sempervivum). All can survive drought conditions, but will sulk in damp or shade.

Roots can be adapted in a variety of ways as well. The swollen roots of kniphofias, agapanthus and dieramas (all South African natives) are adapted to survive for six dry months and six damp months. Some sun-loving irises, bulbous alliums, tuberous dahlias and tap-rooted eryngiums survive by using their own underground water tank.

Gravel gardens need a more dramatic style of planting than the traditional cottage garden border and the backbone of mine is provided by grasses and grass-like flowering plants. Grasses subdivide themselves into two main categories: early-season and late-season. To generalize, the late-season grasses (such as miscanthus, molinia and calamagrostis) flower in autumn, providing a good winter silhouette, and tend to like moisture-retentive soil. The early-season grasses (festuca, most stipas and helictotrichon) favour drier conditions and give a good seedhead until late summer.

Two grasses unify the gravel garden here by providing an 'optic-fibre lamp' presence throughout the year. The aptly named ponytail grass (*Stipa tenuissima*) dries to a shade of bleached canvas in late summer and remains like that for months. Then in late spring it sends up hundreds of tiny green threads before it starts to bleach and fade again. It's a wonderful sight when these filaments (I can't call them leaves) catch the raindrops. This grass only grows to 24 inches (60 cm) in height and it's long-lived here.

Stipa tenuissima

Brown carex provides the same presence. They look, to some eyes, like dead grasses for much of the year – and I try to weave these through the gravel as well. They are wonderful in winter – warm moving swards in soft brown. In spring with an underplanting of blue *Anemone blanda* they make a shining sight. *Carex buchananii* is an upright brown sedge which has leaves that corkscrew at the ends. *C. comans* bronze has fine leaves that spiral out from a tight waist and *C. flagellifera* is more olive green in colour. They survive on dry soil – with my gravel mulch – but would probably prefer richer soil.

These shorter grasses and sedges flutter at ground level – even in winter. The more dramatic grasses – the ones that reach over 36 inches (90 cm) – are deciduous and send up their new shoots in late March or April. Of these, silver feather grass (*Stipa barbata*) has the biggest wow effect on visitors to my garden. This grass has long silky awns up to 12 inches (30 cm) in length and the soft colour of maize haulms. The seed is sharp and pointed – and designed to spear the soil. Damp weather sees

the seed, once it's on the ground, spiral tightly and this corkscrew turning pushes the seed into the ground. On a breezy summer's day, the whole plant looks like Goldilocks – the long blonde tresses softly streaming through the air. By late summer, the seeds have dispersed. They can be hazardous if you have pets or young children and the plant has a tendency to be short-lived.

The golden oat grass (*Stipa gigantea*) is taller, but less dramatic. This makes a shimmering golden screen – of 6 feet (1.8 metres) or so – between the gravel garden and the autumn border. The seedheads stay in good condition until late into the year, like huge wild oats. Two other feathery stipas, *S. capillata* and *S. elegantissima* also grow in the gravel. Both reach 24–36 inches (60–90 cm) high and flower in midsummer.

One of the reasons I wanted to create a gravel garden here is that I knew it would enable me to grow angel's fishing rod (*Dierama pulcherrimum*). For most of the year this looks like a grass with its strappy green leaves, but in

late June it sends up wiry stems of papery buds. They open – some bright pink and others paler – over several weeks in July, finally producing a string of arching bells. The delicate flowers seem able to withstand the heaviest rainfall; they're the plant equivalent of a ballet dancer – superficially fragile but with the inner strength of tensile steel. Once the flowers fade, the bobbly seedheads remain to tremble and move over the garden for many months.

I allow the seeds to drop. All my flowering plants were started by scattering seeds from other people's dieramas and it took about four years for them to get to flowering size. Seven or eight years later I can rely on almost fifty arching flowerheads swaying over the summer garden. Later, in the autumn, the movement continues when *Gaura lindheimeri* 'The Bride' sends up slender wands of white flowers. One cultivar, *G.l.* 'Whirling Butterflies', describes the light, airy nature of this plant with its trembling flowers.

Also in late summer the slender, ramrod-straight *Verbena bonariensis* produces flat heads

good shape through much of the autumn. The whole plant reaches 36 inches (90 cm) in height and will also grow and flower in deep shade.

The shorter and stiffer *E.bourgatii* 'Picos Blue' produces a spike of bright blue flowers set against finely divided leaves in midsummer, reaching barely 24 inches (60 cm) in height. By late summer the thin-stemmed, willowy *E. planum* produces electric-blue stems and tiny branches of round, strokeable heads. This plant tends to lean about. My ultimate favourite among the perennial eryngiums is an old cross called *E. × zabelii*, a plant with true-blue feathery bracts and marbled leaves. It usually precedes the dieramas. *E. alpinum* 'Superbum' is amethyst blue with three rows of bracts surrounding a strokeable thimble. Amethyst blue is very hard to place in the garden and, while 'Superbum' rarely lives for long here, *E. × zabelii* is a real survivor.

of deep purple flowers. This is another weather-resistant performer – able to survive monsoon-like downpours unscathed. This short-lived perennial reappears after most winters in the gravel garden and self-seeds a little. I raise new plants in the greenhouse every year as this butterfly favourite has the ability to float over the gravel – about 36 inches (90 cm) above the surface. In better soil, it grows taller. Self-seeding is a hit-and-miss affair here and I can't bear to be without this verbena.

The eryngiums, angular plants with metallic ruffs, make a bold statement in the gravel. The seeds of the biennial *E. giganteum* germinate straight into soil or gravel during winter and soon make long tap roots, enabling them to flower in the second year. The seeds are best sown in the ground – rather than in pots – and I leave four or five seedheads intact, removing the rest. The very prickly seedheads can be dried for indoor use; they fade to bleached canvas and keep a

The most substantial plant in the gravel garden is a 4 foot (1.2 metre) high pink cornflower with enormous papery buds held on stiff stems. *Stemmacantha centaureoides* (formerly *Centaurea* 'Pulchra Major') has grey-green divided leaves and, as the flowers open, each pale straw, scaled bud forms a head reminiscent of a Red Square onion dome. Then the tufts of blue-pink flowers break through the bud. After several years, I can hope for over thirty flowers and yet I rarely see this plant elsewhere.

By the end of summer a warm red kniphofia called 'Prince Igor' will tower above everything – topping 6 feet (1.8 metres). These two plants are milestones in my gardening year: the stemmacantha tells me summer's really here and the torches of 'Prince Igor' signal its end.

From left *Stipa barbata; S. gigantea;* dierama

The dark-leaved sedums come into their own during late summer. The low-growing 'Vera Jameson' and the very similar 'Bertram Anderson' have dark leaves and bright pink flowers. The wine-red *Sedum telephium* subsp. *maximum* 'Atropurpureum' has purple-brown leaves and stems throughout summer, whereas some of the darker sedums only colour up later in the year.

A carpet of several hardy geraniums softens the whole area throughout summer. The tiny leaves of *G. harveyi*, a South African geranium, are soon topped with mauve-pink flowers. The taller, woodier *G. robustum* has very divided leaves and larger purple-pink flowers. These two seem to be hardy in gravel and produce some interesting hybrids. 'Philippe Vapelle' – a hybrid between *G. renardii* and *G. platypetalum* – produces mid-blue veined flowers against grey-green scalloped leaves.

G. pratense 'Mrs Kendall Clark' is a stiff upright hardy cranesbill with lavender flowers veined in white. This produces a mass of seed

(that comes true) and needs deadheading to avoid too many seedlings appearing in the gravel. By deadheading, you will keep it in flower over several weeks. 'Ann Folkard' and 'Salome' finish the season. Both have the scrambling *G. procurrens* in their gene bank and 'Ann Folkard' produces magenta flowers with a black eye in full sun, whilst 'Salome' likes the shade and sends up smoky purple flowers.

Leafy artemisias – 'Lambrook Mist' and *A. ludoviciana* 'Silver Queen' – creep through the gravel. Rock roses (*Helianthemum* 'Wisley Primrose' and 'Chocolate Blotch'), a sulphur-yellow helichrysum, ballotas and two sages (*Salvia officinalis* 'Berggarten' and 'Purpurascens') add to the silver haze.

French lavender (*Lavandula stoechas*) provides some of the earliest flowers. The trick with this is to trim it back lightly after the first flush of flower (usually in May) and then deadhead it throughout the summer. This will keep it in flower for months. 'Willow Vale' is a

fine mauve with a crinkled tuft, 'Helmsdale' burgundy purple and 'Fathead' a dark purple. The purplish heads are flattered by a backdrop of pale yellow daisies provided by *Anthemis tinctoria* 'E.C. Buxton', 'Sauce Hollandaise' and the earlier hybrid Susanna Mitchell ('Blomit'). Hardy lavender (*Lavandula angustifolia* and *L. × intermedia*) can cope with and thrive on a severe August chop, but more tender lavenders need a gentle trim after the first flowers have faded. Cutting them back hard will surely kill them.

Most silver plants have Mediterranean habits: they grow in wet winters and tend not to be long-lived by nature. As an insurance policy, keep several large pots of moist horticultural sand in a shady place and every time you trim or break a piece from a silver-leaved plant stick it straight into the sand (with a label – I say this with feeling!). It will root in weeks and can be

potted up in half sand, half compost and transferred to the garden during the next spring.

My favourite combination in the whole garden is a carpet of a creamy-white, silver-leaved spreading achillea (*A. nobilis* subsp. *neilreichii*) surrounding a tall magenta pink called *Dianthus carthusianorum* or Carthusian pink. This green-leaved dianthus (more reminiscent of a sweet William than a pink) produces clusters of dark buds and bright single flowers, followed by dark seedheads over many months. The combination of cream and dark pink has real eye appeal.

Dianthus of every type do well in open sunny, well-drained borders. The spicy-clove scent of several of the single varieties is always uplifting and, as with all the other plants I've mentioned, you'll never need a watering can or a hose. These plants depend on a spell of hot, dry weather.

Above from left *Kniphofia* 'Percy's Pride'; *K.* 'Prince Igor'; *K.* 'Wrexham Buttercup'; *Geranium harveyi*; *G. robustum*; *Dianthus* 'Elizabethan'

THE MOTH

There are 2,000 species of moth in Britain, and most are nocturnal. Some are well-known garden pests – the codling moth, for instance; others, though, are beautiful. Moths are far more numerous than butterflies, but they are much less noticeable as many appear as darkness falls. The moth is an important pollinator and some plants – the soapwort and campion, for instance – produce nectar late in the day so as to attract them. The pollination is entirely accidental – as it is with the butterfly. The insects are looking for nectar and transfer pollen to other flowers in the process.

   Moths are attracted by night-scented flowers in pale colours – whites and lilacs. Day-flying moths, and this includes the hawk moths, also like nectar-rich flowers and the dianthus is one of their favourites. The following plants are highly popular with moths here:

Oenothera stricta

Red valerian (*Centranthus ruber*)
Sweet rocket (*Hesperis matronalis*)
Lady's smock (*Cardamine pratensis*)
Honeysuckle (*Lonicera periclymenum*)
Tobacco plants (*Nicotiana*)
Phlox
Garden pinks (*Dianthus*)
Bladder campion (*Silene vulgaris*)
Evening primrose (*Oenothera*)
Verbenas
Soapwort (*Saponaria officinalis*)
   – especially the single form

Moths use the following plants as food plants – the caterpillars eat the leaves. Different species use specific plants: clarkia, ash (*Fraxinus*), fuchsia, poplar (*Populus*), lime (*Tilia*) and willow (*Salix*).

Right *Lonicera periclymenum* attracts moths during early evening, when it is at its most fragrant.

AUTUMN

CHAPTER TEN

The Jewel-box Effect

DON'T TAKE ORGANIC WASTE OUT OF THE GARDEN
— USE IT FOR COMPOST

The first bout of cutting back and tidying is upon us. All those stems and leaves you cut down should be used to replenish the garden soil. You can shred them or compost them – it's up to you. If you opt for a shredder, you can feed the dry plant material straight in (with the seedheads removed if desirable) and tip it back on to the border to form a mulch and feed. If this isn't possible, you can add the shreddings to the compost heap and leave them to rot down. These small chippings will decompose very rapidly. Shredding damp slippery plant material is a frustrating business, so choose dry weather. British gardeners have been slow to take to the shredder, but the pressure on landfill sites will eventually mean that we'll all have to own one – or use a local council facility. Very green material is best left to dry for a week and then shredded. Soft leafy plants jam the shredder.

Compost improves the soil structure as well as replenishing nutrients. That makes for better growing conditions – leading to healthier plants. This soil-conditioning process can never be emulated by adding a 'sprinkle-on' fertilizer, as the real value of compost is its airy, friable nature. This helps root development and the trapped air keeps the soil warm.

Compost – the nitty-gritty

Whole books have been written about compost heaps – but not by me! In fact there is no mystery or great complicated science involved. The secret of a good compost heap is to understand the process involved and to realize that there are two types of compost heap – cool and hot.

Most gardeners make a 'cool' compost heap by adding plant debris to the heap (or bin) throughout the year. I like to use square wooden bins with an open top. I have three, and this is ideal as it means I can transfer material from

Previous page *Aster novae-angliae* 'Primrose Upward' attracts a peacock butterfly.
Left A garden warbler devoured the winged male ants on this *Persicaria amplexicaulis* 'Firetail' seconds after I took this photograph.

one to another. I dig the compost out once a year, usually in late spring. These heaps don't generate a huge amount of heat, but after a year the bottom layer is ready to dig. And as this compost hasn't been subjected to consistently high heat (it might have been very hot in the middle but cooler on the edges) it's better to use it in trenches and at the bottom of planting holes. If you spread it across the surface, you run the risk of the seeds within the compost germinating – and some of them will be weeds. Don't spread it over your borders, unless you're prepared to weed for a year.

Making a hot heap takes more effort, but the compost will be ready in six weeks and this compost is guaranteed to be weed free, as the process involves high temperatures. Making it requires gathering together enough fresh plant material to make a heap in one go – so this is an option for gardeners with larger gardens or vegetable patches.

Chop up all the stems with shears or a shredder and mix them together before they go on to the heap. Lightly place the plant debris in a bin to leave as much air available as possible. I don't cover mine. Within a few days, the heap will feel warm to the touch. When you feel the heap beginning to cool, tip out the contents and remake the heap. The knack is to get the outside (the less rotted material) into the centre of the bin. Repeat this step several times until the heap reaches a constant temperature. Having two bins side by side makes this a much easier process.

Hot compost heaps are definitely for the enthusiast with space and time. The big advantage is that this compost can be used for everything – even growing seeds. You can use temporary willow or hazel structures to make

bins, as the compost only takes a few weeks; some gardeners make a hot heap at the edge of the vegetable patch when the potatoes and other vegetables are being harvested.

The hot heap is so fast because all biological processes produce heat and when more heat is generated than can escape, as in an enclosed compost bin, the temperature rises. As it does, the bacteria which only work – breaking down the material – at low temperatures are replaced by a specialized group of microbes which can tolerate higher temperatures, of up to 80°C (176°F). They have a much higher metabolic rate too, and this enables them to break down plant debris at a faster rate. After this surge of activity in the compost heap, which usually lasts for fourteen days or so, the temperature falls. This allows the heap to be colonized by tiny insects and worms which feed on the partially degraded material, eventually turning it into rich compost.

Moisture plays an important part in compost making too – in both hot and cool heaps. In dry weather, you can add water and keep the moisture in by placing old carpet (something I promise not to mention again) as a cover.

A last flash of brilliance

Before you consign everything to the compost heap, the garden has a last flash of brilliance. September arrives and at the flick of a switch, the garden moves from a tired end-of-summer affair to a serene state peculiar to early autumn. Every plant is flattered by the clear light of September. I can never decide whether autumn flowers are brighter than other flowers or just enhanced and deepened by the extraordinary clarity of the seasonal light. The garden is going through a golden patch and the

Geranium Rozanne, *Malva sylvestris*, red dahlias, *Buddleja* 'Lochinch' and weeping pear (*Pyrus salicifolia* 'Pendula')

heavy dews – brought about by warm days and cool nights – only add to the magic.

My small autumn border shines on two occasions. In May the late single tulips flower amongst the emerging asters, monardas, persicarias and aconitums. I plant the darkly sultry 'Queen of Night' and the clear pink 'China Pink' during November – when the perennials have largely finished. The soil is not much richer than anywhere else in the garden, but this area gets less overhead sun and stays moister for longer – really only drying out in August. The showy, late tulips will tolerate some shade and last longer for being out of full sun.

Shortly after the tulips, several flowering shrubs plug the gap. Ornamental elders produce mostly flat heads of tiny flowers and the dark forms with pale pink flowers – *Sambucus nigra* Black Beauty ('Gerda') and 'Guincho Purple' – are often mistaken for hydrangeas. The golden-leaved S. *racemosa* 'Plumosa Aurea' has very divided golden leaves and lime-yellow conical flowerheads and it brightens up one of the darkest corners at the back of this border. I also use a variegated cultivar, S. *nigra* 'Albovariegata'. Elders have two main advantages: they tolerate poor, dry conditions (once established) and they can be cut down to ground level (stooled) every second or third year. They are fine ornamental plants and don't produce unwanted seedlings or masses of berry. Their clusters of tiny flowers mingle well with perennials. Please, don't let the hedgerow elder put you off these fine garden forms.

Cotinus coggygria 'Royal Purple' provides bursts of large, round, deep red leaves. These are followed by fluffy flowers – if the plant gets sufficient sun. I've woven the lovely blue clematis 'Perle d'Azur' through its branches. I also use fragrant, late-spring viburnums (*V. × juddii* and *V. × burkwoodii*), *Philadelphus* 'Belle Etoile' and the dark *Buddleja davidii* 'Black Knight'. All give me spring and summer flowers before the autumn perennials begin.

I use several cultivars of *Miscanthus sinensis* throughout the autumn border. These mostly tall grasses reach over 5 feet (1.5 metres) and produce airy soft heads during August and September. These heads shimmer in the sun and last through winter – varying in colour from cream (when young) through to deep maroon. In my garden, in the Cotswolds, most flower by September but if you garden in the south or west of England your miscanthus will be a month earlier, at least. Further north, in cold, bleak gardens, they may not produce

flower at all – so experiment with one or two first.

The most established *Miscanthus sinensis* here is an old-fashioned cultivar called 'Silberfeder'. It is often maligned in favour of newer miscanthus. This is my earliest and is always in flower during August, producing lots of graceful heads – some of the others can be rather mean with their flowers.

The shorter 'Kleine Fontäne' reaches 4–5 feet (1.2–1.5 metres). It also produces lots of flowers by late August and their reddish heads pick up the colour of the cotinus foliage near by. Other good forms grown include 'Undine' (a light elegant brownish head), 'Ferner Osten' (a medium-height red), 'Roland' (a giant blond with wavy Afghan-hound hair) and the best red, 'Malepartus'. *Molinia caerulea* subsp. *arundinacea* 'Transparent' produces wonderful winter silhouettes of erect heads with tiny airy seeds that age to dark black, providing some of the best winter seedheads.

With such large grasses the border has to contain some substantial perennials for balance. The tall, black-leaved blue *Aster laevis* 'Calliope' is a stately, easily grown plant reaching 4 feet (1.2 metres) or more and the large blue flowers contrast well with its dark leaves. This lies close to a chocolate-leaved loosestrife called *Lysimachia ciliata* 'Firecracker' – a plant that produces dark leaves from the word go followed by single yellow flowers.

Another bolt of rich, cobalt blue is provided by *Aconitum carmichaelii* 'Arendsii', a monkshood with substantial thick stems and soft leaves and one of the best September-flowering aconitums. (Earlier ones in this border include the silvery 'Stainless Steel', the white and blue *A.* × *cammarum* 'Bicolor', the almond-pink *A. napellus* subsp. *vulgare*

'Carneum' and the two deep blue 'Spark's Variety' and 'Bressingham Spire'.) Blue is a striking colour in any border, as well as a real evening star.

The deep blue of *A. carmichaelii* 'Arendsii' is the perfect partner for the equally tall *Helianthus* 'Lemon Queen'. Though this perennial sunflower makes a huge clump, it doesn't run, and it produces single lemon-yellow daisies with black speckling at the centre. Check carefully the habit of tall yellow daisies – helianthus, sylphium and rudbeckia. Some are thugs, capable of running through an entire border within months.

I encourage stands of *Verbena bonariensis* here. Still on the tall side, but in this case as willowy as any supermodel, it hardly takes up any soil space. It doesn't survive the winter in damp soil, but as I have already mentioned

Above from left *Miscanthus sinensis* 'Silberfeder'; *M.s.* 'Kleine Silberspinne'; low-growing *Verbena hastata* with *Stipa tenuissima*; flowerheads of *Verbena bonariensis*

does come through in gravel. The New York ironweed (*Vernonia noveboracensis*) adds another touch of purple. This moisture-lover is similar in bearing to eupatorium: both produce round heads of flower followed by fluffy seeds. A tall cultivar called *V. crinita* 'Mammuth' will top 7 feet (2 metres).

The tufted flowers of vernonia and eupatorium and the tufted monardas are all stiff-stemmed and contrast well with the moving, fluid grasses. Monardas enjoy moistish soil and sun and can suffer from mildew. The following cultivars are less likely to succumb: the bright red vigorous 'Squaw', the red 'Gardenview Scarlet', the dark purple ' Scorpion', the pink 'Fishes' and the violet-purple 'Prärienacht' have done well here. Their stiff stems and hard, domed heads form a good seedhead long after the whorls of flower have faded.

Another good-value group are the persicarias or knotweeds. In rich soil, *P. amplexicaulis* 'Firetail' would probably be too invasive, but I grow it here. I treat it rather unkindly and cut off the first flush of flowering stems – and then the main flush of flower comes in August, a lacklustre time. The pink cultivar 'Rosea' is very fetching and most forms reach 36 inches (90 cm). The shorter *P. affinis* is a good border edge, but it develops lots of brown foliage through the winter which does not disappear until May.

A new red-leaved cultivar called *P. microcephala* 'Red Dragon' has wine-red leaves marked by a chevron and white flowers. This looks as if it will be a good addition to my garden and has proved hardy here. The newly

Top *Vernonia crinita* 'Mammuth'
Bottom *Eupatorium purpureum* subsp. *maculatum*

bred astrantias repeat flower: *A. major* 'Hadspen Blood' and 'Lars', both deep red; *A.m.* subsp. *involucrata* 'Canneman', a tall pink with green streaking on the outer bract; and *A.m.* 'Roma', a flecked pink. These members of the *Umbelliferae* (the insect-magnet family, now called *Apiaceae*) have a ring of bracts surrounding tiny flowers and they enjoy the shadier edges. The common name of Hattie's pincushion alludes to their delicate charm.

The daisy, really a butterfly landing platform, dominates the autumn border in the form of asters, rudbeckias and echinaceas. Of these, the asters are the most diverse and useful group. Too many gardeners dismiss them, having had childhood experiences of those stiff-stemmed, mildew-ridden monsters. Explore the genus and you will find a whole range of asters, some highly bred and some species. Often they have small airy flowers or lovely foliage, and they don't just flower in September. The key factor in ensuring their survival is dividing them in the spring, not in the autumn.

A. × *frikartii* 'Mönch' is a hybrid between the Italian aster (*A. amellus*) and a long-flowering Himalayan aster (*A. thomsonii*). This difficult cross was made by a Swiss nurseryman called Frikart, who named his plants after Swiss mountains – 'Eiger', 'Mönch' and 'Jungfrau'. The best is 'Mönch'. This healthy, easy plant, tolerant of dry conditions, flowers in late July (here) and produces large, narrow-petalled lavender flowers on stiffish stems (reaching 30 inches/75 cm) until the end of September. The holly-green foliage flatters the lavender of the flower and it's a perfect plant for the front of a sunny border. It will remain in the garden for years, doesn't need regular division and looks good in August!

It isn't the earliest aster to flower. The large white daisies of *A. schreberi* carpet the ground in June, under the shade of the cotinus and the ornamental elders. Its dark serrated foliage emerges early in the year and it grows where most things would struggle – in dry shade. It reminds me of *A. divaricatus* – the white wood

Above from left *Monarda* 'Squaw'; *M. punctata*

aster so loved by Gertrude Jekyll. Both have small white daisies, but the black stems of *A. divaricatus* deviate and twist and turn as the plant emerges. It also likes dry shade and looks best in large drifts. Jekyll famously used it with bergenias in her garden at Munstead Wood. Of the two, *A. schreberi* is by far the more vigorous.

The Italian aster (*A. amellus*) flowers in September, producing floppy flower stems reaching barely 12 inches (30 cm) in height. There are many forms of this species to choose from. 'Veilchenkönigin' (Violet Queen) is the most vibrant, providing lots of smaller richly coloured flowers. Another, 'King George', has larger, earlier flowers. Both Violet Queen and 'King George' are ideal choices in sunny places, but *A. amellus* is not as enduring as *A. × frikartii* 'Mönch' and must always be planted in spring.

The most highly bred asters emanate from two species, either the New York aster (*A. novi-belgii*) or the New England asters (*A. novae-angliae*). Of these two, the New York asters are moisture-loving and succumb to mildew when they get short of water. In my dry garden, I grow the very compact heather-pink 'Coombe Rosemary' and ignore the others.

The New England asters are not prone to mildew and *A. novae-angliae* 'Harrington's Pink' and 'Purple Dome' are two favourites. 'Harrington's Pink' combines grey-green, downy leaves and pure pink flowers, reaching just over 36 inches (90 cm). 'Purple Dome' is a compact, vibrant aster that reaches just under 24 inches (60 cm).

Top *Aster schreberi*
Centre *A. novae-angliae* 'Harrington's Pink'
Bottom *A.* 'Little Carlow' with *Persicaria amplexicausis* 'Firetail'

Some asters wait until October to perform. One of the best of these is *A. turbinellus*, a dry prairie plant. Clouds of small lavender flowers on graceful open sprays make this a lovely addition to the border. It contrasts with the stiffer shape and tiny white flowers of *A. lateriflorus* 'Horizontalis'. Both need some space to shine. If I had to take only one aster to my desert island, though, it would have to be *A*. 'Little Carlow', for this blue aster shines out in any border. It reaches 36 inches (90 cm) in height and is just a mass of intense-blue daisies.

The red pink of the coneflower (*Echinacea purpurea*) blends with asters well. Its sturdy stems and substantial flowers need siting towards the front of the border to be seen to advantage. This plant needs good growing conditions but, being easy to grow from seed, it's a useful plant for gardeners on a budget. Of the named varieties, 'Kim's Knee High' is a short floriferous coneflower and 'Robert Bloom' a strikingly large flower with a lighter, more golden centre. Named varieties don't come true from seed and must be propagated by division.

The rich yellow rudbeckias provide lots of clean-cut yellow daisies with brown-black eyes and some of the shorter perennial forms make wide clumps at the border edges. When buying, beware of the taller rudbeckias – they can be aggressive colonizers and are only suitable for large gardens. All are good in dry gardens. *R. fulgida* var. *deamii* can reach 36 inches (90 cm) in height and has very precise neat flowers. *R. f.* var. *sullivantii* 'Goldsturm' is shorter, the flowers are larger and the ray petals are longer.

Autumn borders allow the gardener to introduce late additions and you can keep

Echinacea purpurea 'Magnus'

some tender plants such as dahlias, fuchsias or salvias in pots and introduce them now to plug the gaps. The golden yellows, deep reds and purples add to the jewel-box richness. The taller dahlias are my favourites. The tall maroon-red Decorative 'Arabian Night', the warm orange Semi-cactus 'Ludwig Helfert', the Decorative Cactus 'Purple Gem' and 'Lilac Time' have all done well here.

You can get two bites of the cherry with dahlia tubers. When they root in late spring in the greenhouse, it's possible to remove one or two strong cuttings from the main plant. Place these in vermiculite, where they will root very quickly, grow them on and plant them out in August. These plants grown from vigorous cuttings do well. You can place the rooted tubers in the border towards the end of May. Remember that if you put out dahlias too early they get a cold shock and don't recover. The taller varieties always need staking and you should do this when planting them. Cut them down after the first frosts and then dig up the

A Japanese anemone in the shade of a buddleja

by perfectly round silvery buds. They open to a clean white and can happily hug the shade. There are strong pink sorts such as *A. hupehensis* var. *japonica* 'Bressingham Glow' and *A.h.* 'Hadspen Abundance'. These plants place themselves, often moving along a border or taking themselves under a path, but they are lovely additions in the autumn gloaming.

As the season draws to an end in late October, some plants (the persicarias, for instance) will demand an autumn tidy-up. Their foliage will be heading towards a soggy mass, helped by frosts. Leave any silhouettes, particularly grasses, to weave their magic during winter. If you want to plant tulips in November you may have to create some space and do a more rigorous tidy.

By creating an autumn border, or including some of these plants, you'll add real September splendour to your garden, allowing you to enjoy those last precious days of the floral calendar. More importantly, you'll be keeping the nectar supply going late into the year, sustaining many insects – and the insects will sustain birdlife.

tubers and dry them off, before putting them into a sturdy box full of dry compost. Place in a frost-free place and check them every month, discarding any mouldy tubers. Replant them in late March. Dahlias can be difficult to grow in cold, wet summers when they can be under constant attack from the gastropods, particularly snails. However, when they do well, they can really inject some life into a border.

The autumn-flowering Japanese anemones (*A. hupehensis* and *A. × hybrida*) can also play a part. The pink cultivars have a tendency to be cool and wishy-washy, but the clean white single *A. × hybrida* 'Honorine Jobert' is a star plant. This nineteenth-century French cultivar has dark green foliage and long stems topped

An old form of Japanese anemone that pre-dates my arrival. The buds are almost better than the flowers.

2211

THE BUTTERFLY

Strangely the presence of butterflies in the garden is at its most spectacular in late summer and early autumn, when numbers of migrants cross the English Channel and head for our gardens. They search for warmth and shelter and dislike windy, exposed gardens. A shelter belt of hedges and trees surrounding a flower-packed border is a must if your garden is to attract them.

Many butterflies – residents and migrants – will mate and lay their eggs in your garden. Most caterpillars feed singly, not in colonies, and won't devastate your plants. The exception is the cabbage white, which has to be kept away from brassicas with netting. The glimpse of a butterfly skimming over the garden before settling on a plant is one of the most uplifting sights in the garden.

Butterflies have long tongues and as they drink the nectar from deep within flowers, they transfer pollen carried on their antennae and heads from flower to flower. They enjoy landing on daisies, flat-headed plants like the verbena and the achillea, and the spikes of the buddleja. Britain has 60 species and about 18 of these will visit a well-stocked garden. Many butterflies are in decline and in order to attract and sustain as many species as possible, gardeners should aim to supply nectar from spring until autumn.

Most widespread butterflies
Large white
Small white
Red admiral
Small tortoiseshell
Peacock

Less widespread butterflies
Brimstone
Green-veined white
Orange tip
Common blue
Holly blue
Painted lady

Comma
Speckled wood
Gatekeeper
Meadow brown

**Butterflies that visit
gardens occasionally**
Small skipper
Large skipper
Small copper
Wall brown
Marbled white
Small heath
Ringlet

Top ten butterfly nectar plants
(identified by the charity Butterfly
Conservation), in order of popularity:

1 Buddleja (*Buddleja davidii*) draws
butterflies like a magnet and a wide
range of species visit it. I like
'Lochinch' with lavender flowers and
grey foliage, but all buddlejas are
popular. It's the most preferred plant
of eighteen species: the brimstone,
comma, common blue, gatekeeper,
green-veined white, holly blue, large
skipper, large white, meadow brown,
painted lady, peacock, red admiral,
small copper, small skipper, small

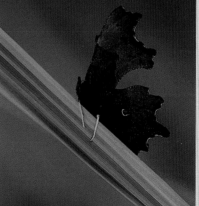

Top A small tortoiseshell on echinops
Centre A comma on a crocosmia leaf
Bottom Small whites mating on a perennial lupin

Buddleja davidii

tortoiseshell, small white, speckled wood and wall brown. It really is a case of every garden should have one!

2 Ice plant (*Sedum spectabile*) – this green fleshy-leaved plant has a flat pink head of flowers during late spring and autumn. All late-summer flowering sedums seem to be attractive to butterflies.

3 Lavender (*Lavandula*) attracts many different butterflies.

4 Asters – *Aster × frikartii* 'Mönch' is one of the best asters, flowering from July until September.

5 Marjoram (*Origanum vulgare*) attracts bees as well as large numbers of butterflies, especially gatekeepers in my garden.

6 Aubrieta – this is an excellent mid-spring and early-summer plant that enjoys growing in cracks and crevices.

7 Red valerian (*Centranthus ruber*) – a real cottage garden favourite. It flowers in midsummer on sunny banks and attracts lots of butterfly species.

8 Field scabious (*Knautia arvensis*) – all scabious are attractive to butterflies.

9 The bramble (*Rubus fruticosus* agg.) attracts thirty species of our native butterfly and can be trained into a hedge. The thornless 'Oregon Thornless' can be trained up a pergola

An orange tip on *Cardamine pratensis*

and is more suitable for small gardens as you won't get torn to shreds when you pick the fruit.

10 French marigold (*Tagetes patula*) – a useful plant when grown close to the vegetable garden, where the strong smell deters pests.

Some of the best food plants for caterpillars

Stinging nettle (*Urtica dioica*) – peacock, small tortoiseshell, painted lady, pale clouded yellow and red admiral.

Golden hop (*Humulus lupulus* 'Aureus') – comma and red admiral.

Grasses – gatekeeper, wall brown.

Lady's smock (*Cardamine pratensis*) and honesty (*Lunaria annua*) – orange tip.

Holly (*Ilex aquifolium*) and ivy (*Hedera helix*) – holly blue.

Violets (*Viola*), clover (*Trifolium*), honeysuckle (*Lonicera*) and pansy (*Viola* × *wittrockiana*) attract rarer butterflies such as some fritillaries.

CHAPTER ELEVEN

Mellow Fruitfulness

I magine being told at the end of September that you can still visit the supermarket, but unfortunately the shelves are going to be empty. This is the situation that many insects and birds face during autumn as the food supply diminishes. Some birds migrate, and others flock together and hunt in packs in order to survive. The natural gardener wants to sustain and keep as many creatures as possible in the garden.

Hedgerows and nearby trees will help, but we can extend the range of food by planting fruiting trees and roses that produce hips. These can be used as specimen plants. Not only do they add winter structure but they provide hibernation sites for many insects, helping to sustain insectivorous birds too.

Hip, berry and haw

The decadent month of September is over; the blowzy flowers are fading. New treasures are emerging, several of the Rugosa roses are full of orange, apple-like hips and the finches are beginning to feed on the seeds. In the wild, *R. rugosa* inhabits the sandy areas of Japan and the roses bred from the species are particularly useful in gardens, not only for their hips. They tolerate poor soil and thrive everywhere, except on chalky or limy soil, which makes the leaves go yellow and chlorotic.

The biggest advantage of Rugosa roses is that they do not succumb to disease; they're probably the most disease-free group of roses. Gallicas, Albas, species roses, Ramblers and Hybrid Musks are also unlikely to suffer from disease. When buying your roses, seek the advice of a reputable rose grower (such as Peter Beales) and ask about disease-free roses. They do exist.

The small, semi-double soft pink rose Bonica ('Meidomonac') is one such rose. Healthy and easy to grow on poor soil, it mixes well with pretty herbaceous plants – such as the annual larkspur 'Earl Grey', asters, phlox and catmints – and it's one of the best roses ever bred. It also produces hips. David

The brilliant red berries of *Ilex* 'J.C. van Tol', a self-fertile holly

Austin Roses has developed a good pink disease-free rose called The Mayflower ('Austilly') and this is proving equally good here, though it's more upright than Bonica.

Rugosas have grass-green foliage and very prickly stems, and they repeat flower. Their fragrant flowers come in shades of white, pink and vivid crimson-purple. Some are single, some semi-double and some truly double. They are useful in the garden and can be grown as specimen shrubs or used to form a hedge. They obligingly tolerate semi-shade and full sun. One, R. 'Roseraie de l'Haÿ', grows under the outer canopy of my large Bramley apple tree to scent the air close to a garden seat.

There are at least eighty named varieties, but the biggest hips belong to 'Fru Dagmar Hastrup', a single pink rose which opens to form a deep cup. The first hips appear by early August, when the rose is still producing lots of flower. The last hips are formed in late autumn and provide seed-eating birds with food in the dark days of winter. In my garden 'Fru Dagmar Hastrup' makes a 4 foot (1.2 metre) high and wide bush.

The taller and much more dressy 'Roseraie de l'Haÿ' has very fragrant semi-double crimson-purple flowers over many months. These hips are redder and not as large – but they seem to be more popular with the birds than 'Fru Dagmar Hastrup', although it may be the position of the rose – it is further away from the house – that makes it a more popular feeding station. The pure white Rugosa 'Blanche Double de Coubert'

Top *Rosa rugosa* 'Fru Dagmar Hastrup'
Centre *R. glauca*
Bottom *R. moyesii*

I find difficult to place in borders, but it is lovely as a single specimen rose or massed together to form a hedge.

The birds also enjoy the flagon-shaped hips of R. glauca, an easy species rose that grows well on my poor soil. This rose can reach 8 feet (2.5 metres), making a branching open shape and the combination of grey-pink foliage and slender, long reddish-brown hips is often put to good use by flower arrangers. The single pink flowers are rather weedy and not attractive in themselves, but the rose is strong enough to stool – to cut hard back. If you do this during spring, the new stems produce larger and darker leaves. The hips on this rose are very popular and have disappeared by November. Bird spillages (from both ends of the bird) ensure that there are always plenty of seedlings under the bush to share around friends and neighbours.

The most dramatic sealing-wax red hips belong to R. moyesii. This makes a large open shrub, easily reaching 10 feet (3 metres) in height. You can use the blood-red flowers at the back of a herbaceous border to great effect. A smaller cultivar called 'Geranium' reaches 8 feet (2.5 metres) and has even larger red hips. 'Highdownensis' is probably the tallest of the three and this produces orange hips. However, all three are large shrub roses and not for small gardens and I have shunned them because of their size and prickliness.

Other specimen shrub roses that form good hips are:

R. 'Complicata' – a single pink with wide flowers up to 5 inches (12 cm) wide.
R. rubiginosa (syn. R. eglanteria) – the very prickly, native sweet briar with apple-scented foliage (which I can only smell after rain) and lots of small single pink flowers followed by oval, red hips.
R. virginiana – an American rose with cerise pink flowers and long-lasting plump red hips.
R. sericea subsp. omeiensis f. pteracantha – a monstrous beauty-and-the-beast rose with translucent red thorns up the stems. Stool to form stunning new growth. Ferny foliage, cream flowers and red hips.
R. macrantha – a trailing rose suitable for banks with single blush-pink blooms and round red hips.
R. macrophylla – a large graceful shrub with clear pink flowers followed by rounded flagon-shaped hips.

These shrub roses need space, but there are several other hip-bearing roses that can be more easily placed in a small garden. The white Rambler 'Wedding Day' produces a cluster of tiny red hips. 'Goldfinch', a Rambler with small apricot-cream flowers, also forms hips. 'Francis E. Lester', a blush-white Rambler, produces clusters of orange hips. 'Madame Grégoire Staechelin', a pink climber that flowers only once, has pear-shaped hips. All can be accommodated against a fence or trellis – but often these hips remain untouched by the birds. Nevertheless, a rose hip rimed with frost is a delight for us during winter, even if the birds aren't impressed.

Ramblers and roses that flower only once are well worth growing because they produce a profusion of flowers and then fade. There's the spectacle of concentrated bloom, with no deadheading, and by adding a late clematis (such as 'Polish Spirit', 'Etoile Violette' or 'Purpurea Plena Elegans') the rose skeleton will have a second flush of flower in late

Our native honeysuckle, *Lonicera periclymenum*

summer – courtesy of the clematis. These small-flowered Viticella Group clematis, bred from a Spanish native *C. viticella*, are drought-tolerant and never suffer from the devastaing clematis wilt.

Climbing roses and some old-fashioned roses may flower throughout the season, but you will need to keep snipping off the flowers as they fade, and they will never drip with bloom in the glorious way the once-a-year showstoppers do. And of course you'll get rose hips only if you leave the spent flowers on.

Hybrid Musks generally make large shrubs, are very healthy and produce lots of flowers from July onwards, often flowering until November. I grow several. The most garden worthy are 'Penelope', 'Cornelia' and 'Felicia'. Of the three, 'Penelope' – a creamy pink – produces the best hips. The soft apricot 'Buff Beauty' is also worth a place in the garden, but it doesn't produce any hips here.

The non-clinging stems of the honeysuckle need a trellis or a wall spanned with sturdy wires for support. The vigorous growth would smother a rose if you planted it with one. Our native honeysuckle (*Lonicera periclymenum*) produces heads of red berries and these are often left untouched by the birds until mid-winter. One year, I had a waxwing, a showy migrant with a seal-pink front and jaunty tuft, feeding on the berries on a freezingly bright January day. Usually it's the blackbirds who gobble them up, though – and they are very grateful.

Forms of *L. periclymenum* are easy to establish within a shelter belt, twining through deciduous hedging. You can easily raise new plants from cuttings taken in early summer or by layering new shoots into the ground to root during spring and summer. These can be moved during the following spring. In the height of summer, during the long evenings, hawk moths will hover over the flowers with their lumbering flight and in the day the bees will drink the nectar.

A west-facing aspect is the most effective wall position for honeysuckles as they hate hot sunshine – it shrivels the buds and they never open. They prefer moist soil and a cool root run and, like the clematis, their upper half scrambles towards the light while the roots skulk in the cool damp down below. If it's difficult for you to arrange these conditions, placing a large container at the foot of the climber will work well, shading the roots.

I grow three forms of this deciduous and sweetly fragrant twiner. The greyer-leaved plain yellow *L.p.* 'Graham Thomas' – discovered in a Warwickshire hedgerow by the late rosarian Graham Stuart Thomas – flowers later than most. 'Serotina' is a darker pink-red cultivar with dark stems and 'Belgica' is a good selection with the traditional rhubarb-pink and custard-yellow flowers.

The American and Chinese honeysuckles have long slender flowers in oranges and yellow, and generally they are not fragrant. They are also demanding, needing a warm site and lots of moisture. I've tucked *L.* × *brownii* 'Dropmore Scarlet' into a shady corner, where it nearly always avoids water stress and the mildew that automatically follows if the plant gets too dry. *L.* × *tellmanniana* is a vigorous

hybrid and easier to grow than the Chinese *L. tragophylla*. Bees are very fond of honeysuckle. Short-tongued bumblebees break into the back of the flower to rob the nectar.

A fruiting tree will attract a whole host of birds to your garden. The robin, blue tit, coal tit, great tit, green and spotted woodpecker, thrush, blackbird and treecreeper have all sheltered in my old Bramley apple tree – often early on a winter's morning. Red admirals have hovered over the fallen fruit on mellow September afternoons and blue tits have collected countless grubs during the nesting season. The tree is the Waterloo station of this garden – and I wouldn't want to be without it.

When choosing apples, it's worth knowing that apples are specific to different areas of the country, varying from county to county. Bramleys thrive all over my village – there are four in different gardens all within a couple of hundred yards – but they may well do badly with you. Sometimes the names of traditional varieties indicate their provenance; the names 'Sussex Mother', 'Bedfordshire Foundling' and 'Keswick Codlin', for instance, tell you all you need to know. Wherever you live, there are apples bred for your soil and climate, and it's worth going to a specialist nursery to find the varieties that grow well with you. The old varieties can be grafted on to a variety of modern rooting stocks, producing a range of heights and habits.

If you own a small garden, you can use espaliers, cordons and small grafted trees, allowing you to grow at least two varieties. This will help to cross-pollinate the crop, which is necessary as most apples are not self-fertile, so growing more than one variety is vital. A lot of the older varieties (including Bramley) are biennial croppers giving a bumper crop one

Crataegus orientalis (syn. *C. laciniata*)

year and a much lighter crop the next. The cropping may influence your choice.

Apple trees do not resent growing in grass, but the plum is a more demanding fruit, preferring open, unplanted ground. The small round greengage, the damson and the plum will all cross-pollinate each other – a very accommodating feature. The self-fertile 'Victoria' is a good choice in a small garden, cropping heavily. Rotting fallers are a magnet for the red admiral and peacock butterflies as well as the birds.

A medlar (*Mespilus germanica* 'Nottingham') here has white scented flowers that appear in May. These are followed by strange brown fruits, which aren't to everyone's taste. The medlar is a very decorative small tree with an interesting crooked shape and the fruits attract the birds. The long-lived and slow-growing mulberry (*Morus nigra*) is also a highly ornamental tree and another magnet for birds and insects. There'll still be plenty of fruit for you, though, and this tree can survive for 500 years, forming a gnarled network of prone trunks. These are both trees I long to plant, given more space, and I have visions of

my great-grandchildren climbing over the low branches of a mulberry I planted. The mulberry was traditionally planted to celebrate a royal visit.

When debating whether or not to plant some fruiting trees, you have to consider the position of your garden, as frost pockets, exposed sites and cold north-facing gardens will never successfully produce trees laden with fruit. You may have to consider planting another type of tree instead, such as the hawthorn or the sorbus. I have never been able to warm towards the berry-laden sorbus. The open flowers smell of rotten meat, the leaves are often large and pinnate, and the berries come in strange shades of coral, yellow and pink. If you like the pinnate-leaved mountain ash style of sorbus get expert, enthusiastic help – don't let me put you off.

I can enthuse about the ornamental hawthorns, though. The downy-leaved intricately cut leaves of the cut-leaved hawthorn (*Crataegus orientalis*, syn. *C. laciniata*) emerge in spring to be followed by creamy white flowers. In autumn the orange-red haws against the silvery foliage are a delight. I'm busy topiarizing mine into a tight lollipop – an idea I first saw in the formal garden at Holker Hall in Cumbria. This small tree could grace any garden with its soft presence, topiarized or not.

The deciduous *C. persimilis* 'Prunifolia' (the white flowers have red anthers and produce lots of fruits, which turn from dark green to glossy red) forms a wide flat canopy, making it an ideal overhead screen for ferns, hellebores and other woodlanders. The shiny round leaves fall early, leaving the branches studded with red haws. *C. laevigata* 'Crimson Cloud', with red flowers with white centres, is another favourite hawthorn. The hawthorns are bone hardy and tolerate wet or dry soil and pollution.

The spindle tree is a euonymus, but quite different from the many cultivars of evergreen shrubby euonymus (*E. fortunei*) most gardeners think of when they hear the name. The spindle tree is a deciduous euonymus that has winged orange and pink fruits during autumn. These are seen against bare branches, as the leaves redden and drop by late September, having provided early (though fleeting) autumn colour.

Spindles harbour the black bean aphid and they are outlawed in North America, but I have never found them a problem in my garden – and I grow broad beans without getting blackfly. There are several good garden forms but, with limited space, I grow just two. *E. planipes,* which forms a V-shaped fountain of a bush, has large substantial leaves that turn deep pink red during early September. The winged fruits and dark stems are revealed as the leaves drop – and all euonymus shed their leaves early. I grow it above ferns and tulips as the exotic foliage seems appropriate. Close by, my three hamamelis also colour up really well. The lovely slow-growing *E. cornutus* var. *quinquecornutus* has six-winged fruits resembling a jester's cap, but this shrub struggles here and is making very slow progress.

If I had more room I would accommodate *E. alatus,* the spindle with corky bark, sometimes forming corky wings along the stems, which has reddish-purple spindle berries and brilliant crimson leaves during autumn, or *E. latifolius,* which produces very large fruits with sharp-edged wings. The most prolific spindle-former of all is *E. europaeus* 'Red Cascade': the branches of this small tree can be weighed down with fruit in September.

Euonymus planipes

The spindle berries disappear during October – probably in the beaks of blackbirds – but the garden value of these euonymus is that they can thrive in dry shade, even in chalky soil. The bark of the spindle – a plant that was once used to make spindles for spinning wool – is very hard and often attractively marked and streaked, and the plant makes a dark, dramatic silhouette during the winter.

Crab apples make excellent trees for small gardens. Many have fragrant flowers, which are a useful source of nectar, *Malus × robusta* 'Red Sentinel' being one of the best, though the fact that the fruits last all winter suggests that they're not very pleasant to eat. Generally, though, the addition of fruiting or berrying plants will sustain more wildlife, add to the shelter and provide autumn and winter interest in your garden – helping you to keep the birds there. Red fruit and berries will also add to the jewel-box richness of an autumn garden.

BIRDLIFE IN THE GARDEN

Puss on the prowl

Over the years my family have flown the nest and each has left me with a cat – and now I am the owner and feeder of three moggies, one belonging to the best beloved. For many years I shunned feeding the birds, convinced that if I attracted more birds into my garden I would simply be confronted by more half-eaten remains.

Research by the RSPB has revealed that birds feeding from a station – a bird table or a particular area in the garden – are safer because they spend less time foraging at ground level. This information prompted me to set up a bird feeding centre with containers of peanuts and black sunflower seeds and now, during winter and spring as I have my morning tea, I watch thirty greenfinches squabble over the seeds and nuts. Coal tits, blue tits, great tits, every other finch, blackcaps and pied woodpeckers have joined in. The sight is delightful and I can confirm that the birds have dodged the moggies far better than they did in most winters.

This supplementary feeding during winter helps many species of bird greatly, but it's important to remember that birds (however well fed) need to breed to survive, and the fledgling birds survive on a diet of insects, not seeds and peanuts. We need to provide a good supply of insects and grubs to feed them as well as a winter supply of fruit, berry and supplementary food. Diverse planting will lure insects into the garden.

One of the best sounds of summer is the rich repetitive song of the thrush. Even better, though, is the smash of a snail shell as a thrush holding it in its beak hammers it on a stone. I place flat stones under shrubs to help them to find a hard surface to use as an anvil – making sure it's well away from Gabby, Sylvester and Puss!

The robin, my gardening companion when I am digging during winter and early spring

The Charcoal Sketch

As autumn slips into winter the natural gardener has to make some realistic choices. If you leave the entire garden alone until spring, the task ahead once spring arrives will be daunting. You'll be far too busy planting seeds, tending the vegetable patch and visiting nurseries; there won't be enough time to tidy the entire garden then.

If you've adopted the Christmas tree approach to planting (where each individual part of the garden lights up for a season before fading to be replaced by another), some areas will contain spring bulbs and flowers. There is no option here: you must meticulously tidy these areas by the end of September – otherwise you'll be flattening the bulbs and plants as you try to tidy in spring. The sensible thing would be to combine spring-flowering plants (hellebores, pulmonarias, snowdrops and wood anemones) with spring-flowering bulbs, giving them their preferred position of dappled shade. Generally I mix daffodils with the woodlanders, and tulips with autumn-flowering plants.

Autumn flowers – especially if combined with winter-silhouette grasses – will give you immense pleasure during early winter. Low sunlight and heavy frost will catch the shapes, picking up intricate details you never noticed in overhead sunshine. You may prefer to wait until February or March before tidying up these areas, but leave it any later and the miscanthus will be too advanced and you may damage the emerging shoots. March is also the best time to divide and replant autumn performers and this isn't always easy if they are among emerging tulips.

The areas that contain mainly summer-flowering plants shouldn't be razed to the ground in autumn as this might well mean many lost plants – cut-down plants are more susceptible to winter cold and wet. Better, if you feel you want a neatening procedure, to shorten the growth by a third, leaving the crown of the plant protected by the long stems and lower leaves during September and then leave the final tidy until late March.

The gravel garden under frost. It is full of Mediterranean plants that keep a presence in winter.

If massive replanning and replanting ready for next year is on the agenda and you have a clay soil, always wait until spring. It will be too wet and cold for small divisions or for plants without a large established root system to survive in cold claggy soil. If your garden is in a frost-free part of Britain and on friable soil, you can get away with a pre-winter haircut without losing any plants to extreme cold or wet, and on that soil planting in September would be desirable.

After examining the evidence and making the all-important decision about what and when to tidy up, once the secateurs have performed a severe autumn crewcut, don't clear away all the debris. Pile some of the stems at the back of the border in a neat heap. These piles will shelter toads, newts, sometimes hedgehogs, ladybirds and other insects. The piles will partially decompose and in late March you can carefully gather them up – although any hedgehogs will need to be left alone. Adding the trunk of a tree or some large logs to a pile will provide shelter and food for the larvae of many beetles.

An intricate picture

Aim to leave parts of your garden intact until early spring. On damp winter days the mass of brown foliage may tempt you to reach for the secateurs. Resist, for when a spell of frosty weather arrives it reveals an intricate picture – a charcoal sketch of seedheads and leaves outlined in silver frost. If the plants have seed-rich heads, the birds will be busy foraging. The sight of a charm of greenfinches raiding the slender heads of the biennial evening primrose on a bright winter's day can be every bit as thrilling as the first rose of summer.

When considering the seedheads of plants, there are two criteria: firstly, how long will the plant stand up during winter (if at all) and, secondly, if I leave the seedhead intact will it become a weed in my garden? The seedheads of the biennial evening primrose (Oenothera biennis), the foxglove (Digitalis purpurea), all poppies, Alchemilla mollis, Welsh poppies (Meconopsis cambrica), teasels (Dipsacus fullonum), aquilegias, Echinops ritro and marjoram (Origanum vulgare) can all be a severe nuisance. These need cautious handling – my advice would be to leave a few, but remove most of the heads after flowering. I also remove most of the heads of all alliums for the same reason. Any plant left to self-seed does so to the detriment of the mother plant, and I usually deadhead prized and long-lived plants too – my special hellebores and my species peonies – to perpetuate the vigour of the choice plant.

Some plants are very short-lived and produce lots of seeds, and you can save these and sow them in the greenhouse or a cold frame. Most perennial seed is best sown straight away – as soon as it's ripe – as it loses viability quickly; but some seeds need a period of vernalization (a cold shock) and are best kept in a frame or a sheltered place outdoors. Patience is a byword with perennial plants – some may take four years to germinate.

Only gather seed on a dry day, preferably at midday, so as to ensure that the seed capsule is dry – this avoids fungal rot setting in during storage. Having snipped off the seedheads with scissors, place them in a paper bag with a written label, and also label the bag. You can keep annual seeds in the bag and then clean them in the winter months (by removing the debris) and place them in a sealed, labelled envelope, again with a label. Keep the envelopes somewhere cool and dry – a biscuit tin in a fridge or a sealed container in a garage or shed. Large seeds (for instance, those of angelica, magnolia and peony) are attractive to mice, so sow these in pots, remembering to net them.

Biennial as well as perennial seeds need immediate attention. Place them on a saucer or tray with a label, clean them on the same day and then plant them – also on the same day if possible. Three inch (7 cm) round pots full of soil-based compost are my preference for sowing all seeds. Time is of the essence, and if you hive these seeds away in a paper bag on a shelf the old adage 'out of sight, out of mind' will apply. Then they won't germinate when you do rediscover them. The big enemy when sowing seeds is damping off, a fungal disease. Using clean pots and trays, and watering with tap water, are the best deterrents. Square pots get damp corners and this can encourage damping off.

Experience will teach you which plants make good outlines. Some plants rule themselves out at the start – most persicarias, for instance – by collapsing in a soggy mess at the first sign of a cold night. Amongst the most enduring heads in my garden are those of the stately bear's breeches (*Acanthus spinosus*). The hooded flowers of this upright, handsome foliage plant produce round seedpods and these will last for months. The ragged bracts that surround them add even more visual appeal in frost. Leaving this plant intact doesn't seem to affect its vigour. This acanthus grows in full sun close to a tall crocosmia (*C. masoniorum*). The sword-shaped, pleated leaves of the crocosmia remain during winter, but it is the old flowerhead, which takes on the branched shape of several birds in flight, that makes it such an attractive winter subject. These two plants remain rigid in most years.

Seedhead of *Acanthus spinosus*

Close to them is a *Phlomis russeliana*, which has heart-shaped silver leaves. It spreads over the ground, so it is probably too invasive for small gardens. The cream and yellow flowers are held on stiff stems in whorls against grey-green felty leaves. These heads are often spaced up the stems and it makes a lovely shape during winter. This ground-hugging phlomis has a large advantage over the shrubbier woody types: it retreats underground at the end of the growing season and is not severely affected in harsh winters. *P. fruticosa*, which also has good heads, can be severely cut back by hard winters and late frosts.

This border, which spans the path close to the vegetable patch, catches the light and the frost, and contains tall southernwood (*Artemisia abrotanum*) a stiff-stemmed, grey-leaved plant that has an aromatic winter presence. *Achillea*

Seedheads of *Crocosmia masoniorum*

The whorled seedheads of *Phlomis russeliana*

'Moonshine', a silver-leaved lemon-yellow achillea flowering from May to October, holds up well for the first half of winter. I leave intact the tiny drumstick heads of *Allium sphaerocephalon* – reaching 24–36 inches (60–90 cm) – among the spires of spent penstemons, purple sage (*Salvia officinalis* 'Purpurascens'), dianthus, rock rose, catmint and verbascum. The spire of the acanthus, lightened by the multi-branched crocosmia and framed by all the other textures, is every bit as wonderful on a frosty winter's day as it is in the height of summer.

In the gravel garden the seedheads of dierama sway above the Mediterranean plants. I usually cut back and tidy these in February – weather permitting. You need gloves when handling dieramas as they produce long splinters of leaf. You should always leave the branching candelabras of *Verbascum bombyciferum* intact until the last moment; you can tap their seeds out of the head, sprinkling them where you want them, before consigning them to the compost heap.

I also leave the main cottage garden intact. One of the best heads there belongs to the modest fennel (*Foeniculum vulgare*), a 36 inch (90 cm) high plant with finely cut, aniseed-flavoured leaves and delicate umbels. Though by autumn the seeds have long gone, the ribs of the umbel make a delicate lacy head. This pops up amongst another crocosmia, the fiery red 'Lucifer', providing me with one of my favourite combinations in summer and winter. The seedhead of 'Lucifer' is rather plain and nowhere near as enduring as *C. masoniorum*, but fennel heads keep their shape for months. The spent daisies of echinacea and rudbeckia can be left to disintegrate without any consequence. These contrast well with the spikes of the aromatic *Agastache foeniculum* which comes through in most winters. All agastaches are easy from seed and flower in their first year. A dark purple teucrium (*T. hircanicum*) also provides black spiky heads against the crinkly leaves. The ultimate spike is provided by veronicastrums, but only one grows well here – 'Pointed Finger', which has pink horizontal 'fingers'. As a tribe these late-summer flowering plants need a high water table. Those of you with alluvial soil on low land should grow them – Dutch gardeners use them to stunning effect.

Sedums can be enjoyed by all as they are not demanding plants to grow. When the late summer flowers fade, they are replaced by a dark seedhead. The old garden favourite *Sedum* 'Herbstfreude' (Autumn Joy), has green leaves and deep pink flowers, and forms a large flat, indestructible brownish-red head. Although butterflies love this plant and in winter it forms the best sedum head I know, I have defected and only grow sedums with dark or glaucous foliage. *S. telephium* subsp. *ruprechtii* provides pigeon-grey leaves; *S.t.* 'Matrona' has huge fleshy leaves in pinkish grey darkening to red; and *S.t.* subsp. *maximum* 'Atropurpureum' makes a lovely dark feature by late summer with its dusky purple leaves – and the rosy pink flowers gradually fade to dark chocolate brown. All sedums are late nectar plants, too.

On the outer edges of the garden, three tall plants draw in the goldfinches. The humble teasel (*Dipsacus fullonum*), a biennial, has prickly domed heads that are now brown. As the seeds form, the goldfinches descend to feed. The plant is not for the small garden, but ideal for the outer edges in largish plots, though you will have to be ruthless in April and prize out any unwanted self-seeders. The leaves, which are perfoliate, form a useful reservoir for rainwater and I have often seen the birds drinking the water cupped between the stem and leaf.

The milk thistle (*Silybum marianum*) has mottled foliage – the common name 'Mary-spilt-the-milk' describes the white splashing and veining – and the rosette is a very good winter feature. The pink-purple thistles appear in early summer and by September the black seeds have all but disappeared. This, like the teasel, will self-seed, placing itself where it pleases. Both reach 4–5 feet (1.2–1.5 metres). The leaves are seriously prickly on this one, though.

The giant scotch thistle (*Onopordum acanthium*) is a soft summer plant of great stature. Often seen on the roadside, it has hairy silver-white leaves, downy stems and pale purple flowers. I grow seeds of it in the greenhouse every year. As with all biennials, the rosette has to overwinter. In wet cold winters I lose many of my rosettes – but I still love to see it in full flight.

Some more sun-loving plants with good seedheads

Achillea filipendulina 'Gold Plate' – a tall, stiff-stemmed bright yellow achillea, reaching 5 feet (1.5 metres) or more. Many achilleas make good heads, but this has the largest.
Russian sage (*Perovskia atriplicifolia*) – a branching silver-leaved plant with blue spikes of flower.
French lavender (*Lavandula stoechas*) – the stiff stems and old heads make a short bushy outline.
Eryngium planum – a small-headed eryngium. It

can self-seed a little too enthusiastically.

Origanum laevigatum – the willowy stems have dark purple flowers followed by black seedheads and seeding isn't a problem. 'Herrenhausen' is probably the best.

Verbena bonariensis – the slender purple heads form long-lasting flat heads that retain their shape during winter.

Others flowers for the autumn border

Aster – most can be left intact, but the *A. novae-angliae* varieties can produce unwanted seedlings.

Monardas – all form stiff-stemmed heads.

Anemone hupehensis and *A.* × *hybrida* – these autumn-flowering anemones lose their petals but keep the slender stems and the round centre of the flower.

Phlox – the seedheads can be left intact.

Grasses for winter presence

Miscanthus sinensis – soft wavy heads fading to silver.

Switch grass (*Panicum virgatum*) – upright grasses, some with red-brown colouration, and branching beaded spikelets.

Molinia caerulea subsp. *arundinacea* 'Transparent' – tiny beaded black heads on straight stems.

Pheasant grass (*Stipa arundinacea*) – for moister soil. Has a leafy winter presence and fine thread-like seedheads. The seedhead disintegrates quickly, leaving a floppy leafy grass. It self-seeds in damp soil and is not hardy in very cold winters, but it is useful in dank spots.

Stems

The garden's winter structure can also be enhanced by a number of shrubby plants – straight stemmed or intricately curled. The slow-growing contorted hazel (*Corylus avellana* 'Contorta') makes a tall shrub after ten years or more and produces intricate twists and turns. In winter, each bend catches the raindrops most beguilingly. The catkins brighten up February – surely the grimmest month – and combine well with an underplanting of orange species crocus. It needs careful placing though, for if ever there was a Jekyll and Hyde plant, this is it. The beauty of its winter silhouette is undeniable but the tousled leaves in summer are an ugly sight. And yet it's no good tucking this in a hedgerow, as it needs the backdrop of a wide blue sky. I've set it in lawn in the middle of the cottage garden, where the colour of the cottage border draws the eye away from it during summer. 'Contorta' is grafted on to ordinary hazel stock and has a habit of sending up whip-straight suckers from the bottom of the trunk. These need removing.

The contorted willow (*Salix babylonica* 'Tortuosa') is another plant that is good for its twisted stem, though it is too large for most gardens; and if you've space plant it away from borders and vegetable patches as a willow sucks the moisture from the ground like a sponge.

Ramrod-straight stems in reds and olive green can be effective if several plants of the same type are grouped together. Mixing the groups together works well – giving drifts of red and green. The following dogwoods have good stems and where the stem is straight and vigorous, you can stool (reduce the old stems to ground level) every second year (during April) without harm:

Cornus sericea 'Flaviramea' (syn. *C. stolonifera* 'Flaviramea') – the straight mustard-yellow stems age to olive green and glow in winter light. Produces suckers.

Red-barked dogwood (*C. alba*) – 'Sibirica' has the best red stems, but is less vigorous than

Miscanthus

Corylus avellana 'Contorta'

some red-stemmed varieties; there is also a variegated form. 'Elegantissima' has leaves mottled in white and reddish stems. 'Spaethii' has golden variegated leaves and reddish stems. 'Aurea' has golden leaves and good red stems. 'Kesselringii' has black-purple stems.

The following twiggy-stemmed dogwoods need a careful thin and will not thrive on a savage cut-back:

C. sanguinea 'Midwinter Fire' – robust branching dogwood with orange-pink stems.
C. stolonifera 'Kelseyi' – a dwarf form with a dense habit and shoots of yellow and green with red tips.

These plants tolerate damp, cold places, and when seen against a pond their reflections add another dimension. The idea is to encourage the young vibrant growth and to be able to see the effect from afar. All are good in damp soil.

If space is not a problem, the ornamental blackberries or ghost brambles are a lovely addition to a garden – but (unless you're masochistic) only for the outer reaches. The most vigorous, *Rubus cockburnianus*, has dark stems with a white bloom and each suckering stem curls over at the tip. It is good set in grass in a large garden. Less vigorous is the fern-leaved *R. thibetanus* 'Silver Fern' – this reaches 4–5 feet (1.2–1.5 metres) and has thinner stems. These, like the cornus and willow, should be stooled in April.

Several willows, always good planted by water, could also be used in the larger garden. They include scarlet willow (*Salix alba* subsp. *vitellina* 'Britzensis'), which has bright orange new growth. Violet willow (*S. daphnoides*) has young purple stems with a white bloom and grey pussy willow buds.

If you can give your garden, however small, this sort of winter form and presence in some areas you will avoid that bare 'put-to-bed' look and make the garden an attractive shelter belt and feeding station for your helpers.

SPIDERS

Spiders belong to a group that includes scorpions, mites and daddy-long-legs. They are not insects. All have four pairs of legs and two sections to their bodies. There are approximately 75,000 species of spider worldwide and probably a thousand species in the UK – though the figures are hazy. A study made in south-east England during the 1930s discovered that there were 2 million spiders per acre in an undisturbed meadow. There are 300 species of money spider in Britain alone.

It's a lovely thought that in my ⅓ acre (0.12 hectare) plot I might have half a million spiders – but it's difficult to imagine, as they are so hard to spot. When you do see spiders, they are the most important indicators of a successful organic garden: spiders are susceptible to sprays and soon affected by pesticides and a lot of spiders means that there is plenty of food to support them.

We must view spiders as our friends as these predators catch and eat insects – both friends and foes. On balance they are an important part of the natural gardener's armoury against pests. Some have speculated that spiders are the most important predators in the garden. Each species has its own niche or habitat – for example, one species might spin its web solely by open water, another in shrubs and a third on grass. Gardens with undisturbed areas of leaf litter, shrubby plants, trees and a large range of flowering plants will attract more species.

Only the larger, more obvious ones such as the garden spider come to our attention. But there are also wolf spiders that do not make webs but scurry over low vegetation and bare ground, actively hunting their prey; tiny jumping spiders that leap on to insects; night-hunting spiders that only a dedicated arachnologist would ever see; and crab spiders that live in flowers – often taking on the colour of the flower – and lie in wait for their prey, an unsuspecting pollinator, to come along.

Spider facts

Usually only one generation of spiders is born per year, so it takes time for an effective population to build up. They lay their eggs in autumn, in batches tucked away in nooks and crannies, under stones or behind flakes of bark – in places where the adult spiders also overwinter. Young spiders feed on small insects, graduating to larger ones as they grow. Some spiders live on vegetation, but others such as hunting spiders make their home in mulch, or the thatch of rough grass, and hunt for food on the plants growing above, moving up and down the stems as if they are going off to the corner café for lunch.

A spider sheltering in a *Convolvulus althaeoides* flower

Index

Page numbers in *italic* refer to illustrations